MAITLAND

A Critical Examination and Assessment

by

H. E. BELL

LATE FELLOW OF NEW COLLEGE, OXFORD

HARVARD UNIVERSITY PRESS

Cambridge, Massachusetts

1965

FIRST PUBLISHED 1965

LIBRARY OF CONGRESS CATALOG CARD NUMBER:
65-25077

PRINTED IN GREAT BRITAIN
BY W. & J. MACKAY & CO LTD, CHATHAM, KENT

PUBLISHER'S NOTE

The author died shortly after he had completed this book,
which Miss Betty Kemp of St Hugh's College has kindly seen
through the press. She has collated the references to Maitland's
letters with the Selden Society's volume of his correspondence,
edited by Mr C. H. S. Fifoot, of which a copy was generously
made available to her by Mr Howard Drake of the Society
before its publication.

CONTENTS

ABBREVIATIONS

A.H.R.   *American Historical Review.*

B.I.H.R.   *Bulletin of the Institute of Historical Research.*

B.N.B.   *Bracton's Note Book*, 3 vols. (1887).

Bod., F.P.   Bodleian Library, Fisher Papers.

C.H.   *The Constitutional History of England* (1908).

C.H.J.   *Cambridge Historical Journal.*

C.P.   *The Collected Papers of Frederick William Maitland*, 3 vols. (1911).

C.U.   Cambridge University Library.

D.B. & B.   *Domesday Book and Beyond* (1897).

E.H.R.   *English Historical Review.*

E.L.Ren.   *English Law and the Renaissance* (1901).

Essays.   *Selected Historical Essays of F. W. Maitland*, chosen and introduced by Helen M. Cam (1957).

H.E.L.   *The History of English Law before the Time of Edward I* (1st ed. 1895, 2nd ed. 1898).

L.Q.R.   *Law Quarterly Review.*

Letters.   *The Letters of Frederick William Maitland*, ed. C. H. S. Fifoot (1965).

M. de P.   *Memoranda de Parliamento* (Records of the Parliament holden at Westminster on the 28th Day of February, 1305).

P.R.O.   Public Record Office.

R.C.L.   *Roman Canon Law in the Church of England* (1898).

Sketch.   *Frederick William Maitland, a Biographical Sketch*, by H. A. L. Fisher (1910).

T. & B.   *Township and Borough* (1898).

T.R.H.S.   *Transactions of the Royal Historical Society.*

V.C.H.   *Victoria County History.*

I

THE CHARACTERISTICS OF MAITLAND'S WORK

HISTORIOGRAPHY—the study of the ways in which men have applied themselves to the problem of writing history—has become a fashionable, perhaps too fashionable, subject. For the professional, in history as in any other craft, there must always be an interest in seeing how the greatest practitioners have gone about their business; but whether that interest is sufficient to justify the mass of work that has recently appeared on historiography is not so certain. In particular, an extended study of an individual historian would seem to be justifiable only in one of two circumstances: he must either have been, in some sort, a public figure in his own age, whose historical writing influenced political action of his time,[1] or alternatively he must have introduced and developed ideas and techniques of permanent significance in the writing of history.

Clearly it is not under the first head that a book about F. W. Maitland can be excused, for his is not the historical writing of a Macaulay or a Churchill, interwoven with a public, political career. One of his pupils—Alston, who produced the definitive edition of Sir Thomas Smith's *De Republica Anglorum* —was visiting Maitland at the time when he was engaged on the *Life of Leslie Stephen*, and by a slip of the tongue made a remark about the Life of *Maitland*. "A life of Maitland—I don't think that *that* would take up much space," was Maitland's reply.[2]

Nor, at any rate for our purposes, need it. The outlines are

---

[1] For some seventeenth-century examples see David C. Douglas, *English Scholars 1660–1730* (2nd ed. 1951); J. G. A. Pocock, *The Ancient Constitution and the Feudal Law* (1957).

[2] 4 June 1909, Alston to Fisher, Bod. F.P., Box 27.

simple and the story all too short, though it is not lacking in liveliness, in courage, and in marked sweetness. "I am getting to admire him so much", Maitland confessed when he came to write Stephen's Life, "that I am in danger of becoming a hagiographer."[1] It is perhaps well for me to make a similar admission about my own attitude to Maitland. It is not merely that I regard him as the greatest English historian, but also that (so far as these matters can be judged at second hand, from correspondence and the testimony of reliable witnesses) I admire him as a man of notable goodness and nobility of character and of singularly attractive personality.

Maitland was born on 28 May 1850 in Guilford Street, London. His mother dying the next year and his father a dozen years later, the main responsibility for his upbringing lay with an aunt, his mother's sister, and a series of German governesses who gave him a grounding in the language that was subsequently useful in widening the range of his scholarship—"Blessed be all your German governesses", he wrote, many years later, to his sister.[2] He was at Eton from 1863 to 1869, and from there went on to Trinity College, Cambridge. At Cambridge he ran against Oxford in the three miles race, was successively secretary and president of the Union, and after a false start in mathematics read moral sciences, in which subject, along with his friend William Cunningham, he was elected a scholar of Trinity, and, again bracketed with Cunningham, appeared at the head of the Tripos List. The philosophic interests of this formative period in his life, and in particular the dominant influence of an inspiring teacher, Henry Sidgwick, had permanent effects on Maitland's outlook.

Already in June 1872 he had become a member of Lincoln's Inn, and on his failure to secure a fellowship at Trinity[3] seems to have planned a career at the Bar. He was called in 1876 and

[1] 9 Jan. (1905), Maitland to Jackson, *Letters*, p. 324.

[2] *C.H.J.*, xi, 69.

[3] His dissertation, "A Historical Sketch of Liberty and Equality as Ideals of English Political Philosophy from the time of Hobbes to the time of Coleridge", was privately printed in 1875; it is to be found in *C.P.*, i, 1–161.

spent the next eight years as a conveyancer and equity draftsman, mainly in the chambers of B. B. Rogers and Bradley Dyne. This period proved a significant complement to his Cambridge education, and Maitland himself reckoned it fundamental to his subsequent careeer as a legal historian. "I do not think that an Englishman will often have the patience to study medieval procedure and conveyancing," he was later to say in his inaugural lecture as Downing Professor, "unless he has had to study modern procedure and modern conveyancing and to study them professionally."[1] Yet though there is an important truth in this, the fact remains that there is a wide world of difference between practice at the Bar and the historical studies in which Maitland was to make his reputation. How did he effect the transition from one to the other?

H. A. L. Fisher was no doubt right that Maitland would, in any event, have been drawn to history by the natural workings of his genius.[2] There were, however, influences of a personal sort that are worthy of mention. One such was his accidentally coming across a copy of Stubbs's *Constitutional History*—"I found it in a London club," he wrote many years later in Stubbs's obituary, "and read it because it was interesting."[3] Again, as a member of Leslie Stephen's club, the Sunday Tramps, he was brought into contact with Frederick Pollock, a lawyer of historical interests who was a member of Maitland's own Inn. "I may have done a little to put you on the scent in the days when we first met in Lincoln's Inn", Pollock claimed in 1887.[4] Infinitely more important, however, was Maitland's acquaintance, and subsequent friendship, with Vinogradoff. Their first meeting seems to have taken place at a dinner party given by Pollock in January 1884: the two walked home together and it was then that Maitland confessed to the Russian scholar that he would rather devote his life to the study of English law than wait in his chambers for the footsteps of the client who never comes. As to the conversation between the two, which took place in

[1] *C.P.*, i, 493–494. [2] *Sketch*, p. 22.
[3] *C.P.*, iii, 503.
[4] 9 Nov. 1887, Pollock to Maitland, C.U. Add. MS. 7006.

the Parks at Oxford on 11 May 1884, and from which Fisher, and
indeed in retrospect Maitland himself, dated Maitland's dedica-
tion to legal and record scholarship, Sir Maurice Powicke has
shown that its significance has been exaggerated: the Public
Record Office searchers' register shows that Maitland had indeed
consulted records there on several occasions prior to the meeting
in the Parks.[1] He had published his papers on the Laws of
Wales and the Criminal Liability of the Hundred in 1881, and
on the Early History of Malice Aforethought in 1883, and before
May of the year following he must certainly have been at work
on his *Pleas of the Crown for the County of Gloucester*. Nevertheless
that Vinogradoff helped to stimulate and to inform Maitland's
interests is undeniable: a strong, mutual admiration grew up
between them. Maitland once wrote to Fisher that, were he
Prime Minister, he would risk a European war to put Vinogradoff in the Regius Professor's chair at Cambridge,[2] and
Vinogradoff after Maitland's death wrote movingly of their
association in the days of *Bracton's Note Book* and his own
Villeinage in England.[3]

From the late 'eighties it is even less necessary to our purpose
to follow the chronological story of Maitland's life, for by then
he was well launched on the studies from which his fame derives.
After failing to obtain a readership at Oxford,[4] in 1884 he was
elected into one at Cambridge, the funds for which had been
made available by Henry Sidgwick's beneficent endowment.
Thereafter *Bracton's Note Book*, which appeared in 1887, established his reputation, and the year following he was elected into
the Downing Professorship of the Laws of England at Cambridge. A letter he wrote about his election to Frederick
Pollock, who had been one of the electors, throws a good deal
of light on the characters of the two men. "Your letter from

---

[1] F. M. Powicke, *Modern Historians and the Study of History* (1955), p. 10
note, quoting T. F. T. Plucknett in *L.Q.R.*, lxvii (1951).

[2] 3 Feb. 1895, Maitland to Fisher, *Letters*, p. 130.

[3] P. Vinogradoff, *Collected Papers* (ed. Fisher, 1928), p. 254.

[4] Thomas Raleigh was elected. H. G. Hanbury, *The Vinerian Chair and
Legal Education* (1958), p. 101.

Downing", he said, "tells me what I expected, namely, that the struggle was severe. I can very well understand that there was much to be said against me."[1] The modest misgivings were, of course, unjustified. In the remaining eighteen years of his life Maitland achieved a productivity fantastic alike in its quantity and quality. Apart from the great books, which it will be the purpose of later chapters to discuss, a stream of reviews, papers, introductions flowed from his pen, so that his personal bibliography runs to over a hundred items. Nor was he inactive in university and college affairs—as to the former, he played a notable part in the organization of the Cambridge Historical Tripos;[2] as to the latter, we have a glimpse of him auditing the Downing College accounts.[3] Above all, he saw to it that personal relationships were never crowded out of his life by scholarship. Married in 1886 to Florence Henrietta Fisher, alike at Downing and at Horsepools, the little Gloucestershire manor-house that he had inherited from his grandfather, S. R. Maitland, the church historian, his work was set against a happy domestic background. With his pupils his friendships were close and, though he never admitted to being a letter-writer, he in fact maintained academic correspondence for much of this period with scholars like Round, Bigelow, and his brother-in-law, Herbert Fisher; later, when he was forced to winter abroad, he engaged in a more leisurely correspondence, more general in character, with Cambridge friends such as Henry Jackson and W. W. Buckland.

One final biographical point: all this activity, scholarly and social, took place within the framework of persistent ill health. As early as August 1887 he wrote to Bigelow, "I have been invalided and write this in a Devonshire village where I have been living an animal or vegetable life for some weeks past without law books."[4] The next year he was ill just before

[1] 6 Aug. 1888, *Letters*, p. 46.
[2] Jean O. Mc.Lachlan, "The Origin and Early Development of the Cambridge Historical Tripos", *C.H.J.*, ix (1949), 78–105.
[3] 26 Jan. 1890, Maitland to Fisher, *Letters*, p. 76.
[4] 11 Aug. 1887, Maitland to Melville M. Bigelow, *Letters*, p. 34.

giving his inaugural lecture;[1] more seriously—and it is a comment on the intimacy that had grown up between the two men—he confessed to Vinogradoff frankly in March 1889, "Many things are telling me that I have not got unlimited time at my command."[2] From 1898 it became necessary for him to winter in the Canary Islands, and in these later years his letters contain patient, good-tempered and whimsical references to his sickness. Recognition had not been denied to Maitland—Cambridge, Oxford, Glasgow and Cracow Universities had given him honorary doctorates; Lincoln's Inn had made him a Bencher; on Acton's death he had been offered the Regius Professorship of History at Cambridge. But there was no Indian Summer to his life—only the consciousness of the mass of work to be done and of the short time left to do it. He died at the age of 56.

More important from our point of view than the details of what was essentially a quiet and private life, Maitland's work possessed qualities and characteristics that made it permanently influential on English historical scholarship.

The most obvious of these was its wide range. It is not merely that Maitland's researches stretched from the age of the Saxon settlement to the sixteenth century: it is that within that long period his interests were catholic and his knowledge encyclopaedic. A scholar who is going to write big, wide-ranging books must possess the facility of working quickly. Holdsworth, for instance, did not find it necessary to use accumulated notes, but wrote straight from his authorities,[3] and in this sort of connection Maitland was exceptionally fortunate in having a quite remarkable visual memory: Fisher drew a charming portrait of him, smoking and reading his black-letter law books far into the night, never taking a note, yet being able to retain whatever he wanted.[4] But, of course, the breadth of his scholarship was dependent on

[1] *Sketch*, p. 46.
[2] 12 Mar. 1889, *Letters*, p. 60.
[3] A. L. Goodhart, *Sir William Searle Holdsworth, O.M.*, Selden Soc. (1954), p. 9.
[4] *Sketch*, pp. 178–179.

more than a happy technical facility: it resulted rather from his effort to reconstruct the ideas and motives of the ages that he studied. Because he succeeded so far in this, because, in G. M. Trevelyan's phrase, he "was using mediaeval law as the tool to prise open to our view the mind of mediaeval man",[1] his writings have as much significance for economic, social and constitutional, as for purely legal, history.

Indeed, to describe Maitland simply as a legal historian is inadequate unless the description is accompanied by recognition of the fact that his work utterly changed both the techniques and scope of English legal history. A system like the English common law—

> That codeless myriad of precedent,
> That wilderness of single instances—

in which the principle of *stare decisis* had become basic, was necessarily dependent on history of a sort: few nineteenth-century lawyers would have maintained, as did Sir Edward Clarke, that there was no apparent reason why any law book or document more than forty years old should be preserved.[2] Nevertheless, much that passed for legal history was uncritical. Preoccupation with statement of the rule was rarely balanced by scientific inquiry into the contemporary circumstances that had brought it about; above all, too often anachronisms were perpetrated and comparatively modern concepts imposed where they did not belong, on the law of an earlier age. Nor had the promising start made by the seventeenth-century antiquaries towards the exploitation of the public records been effectively developed, despite the work of the Record Commission. As late as 1888 Maitland wrote to M. M. Bigelow of the Boston University School of Law, "I can't tell why it is, but certainly you seem to care a deal more for legal history on your bank of the Atlantic than we do here. It is a malarrangement of the universe which puts the records in one continent and those who would care to

[1] G. M. Trevelyan, *Autobiography of an Historian* (1949), p. 16.
[2] Sir Cecil Carr, *The Mission of the Selden Society*, Selden Soc. (1961), p. 3.

read them in another."[1] And even in America this interest was
only recent.

The means by which Maitland remedied the inadequacies of
the older legal history, and indeed revolutionized the study of
the subject, are discussed in detail elsewhere in this book.[2] In
the present context, however, it is well to emphasize two
characteristics of his historical writing about law—widely
different from each other, but both probably deriving from his
early philosophical training. The first is his constantly repeated
effort to penetrate to the inner meaning of the words used in his
sources; the second is his eye for the great central concepts of the
common law in different phases of its development.

With regard to the former, Professor R. L. Schuyler is right
to entitle one section of his recent little Maitland Reader "The
Meaning of Words", for, as he claims in his introduction,
Maitland was a pioneer in historical semantics.[3] This is not, of
course, to suggest that he used the technical vocabulary of
semantics (he had technical terms enough, of another sort, on his
hands); on the contrary, his approach to word study was simple,
sometimes it seems almost light-hearted. Frequently his way
into the meaning of a word was through some significant
surviving modern use of it. Thus, seeking to explain the term
sake in the phrase *sake and soke*, he said—"It is still in use among
us, for though we do not speak of a sake between two persons,
we do speak of a man acting for another's sake, or for God's
sake, or for the sake of money."[4] Nor was his approach to the
all-important *seisin* different. "To this day", he reminded his
readers, "we call the person who takes possession of land without
having title to it a 'mere squatter'; we speak of 'the sitting
tenant', and such a phrase as 'a country seat' puts us at the right
point of view."[5] Or yet again, dealing with the *borh*, "the term
borrow", he pointed out, "tells us of a time when men rarely, if

[1] 31 July 1888, *Letters*, p. 45.

[2] Chapters IV and V below.

[3] R. L. Schuyler, *Frederic William Maitland, Historian* (1960), pp. 81–105,
and p. 41.

[4] *D.B. & B.*, p. 84.   [5] *H.E.L.*, ii, 30.

ever, lent without receiving sufficient *borh*".[1] Yet no man was more clearly aware than Maitland of the changing meaning of the same word throughout the centuries, and he took infinite pains to establish the right meaning in a particular context, stressing especially the confusion that might arise when the same word was used in both a general and a severely technical way.[2]

As for his interest in the great concepts of the law, which brought him into the field of jurisprudence, one outstanding example will suffice—his preoccupation with "juristic persons", the trust and the corporation. As early as 1890 he wrote to Pollock about this—"for six weeks past I have had 'juristic persons' on my mind, have been grubbing for the English evidence and reading the Germans, in particular Gierke's great book".[3] His studies on this topic informed much of what Maitland wrote on the borough; they led to his translation of Gierke's *Political Theories of the Middle Ages* in 1900, and in the years just after the turn of the century to a notable series of original papers.[4] At one stage he proposed "Hic jacet persona ficta" for his own epitaph.[5] Much of Maitland's most subtle scholarship was turned on to this work: as W. W. Buckland claimed, he was "at his best where law and philosophy meet".[6]

For the common law, on the history of which he had spent so much of his effort, Maitland came to have an admiration that was akin to love. About its achievements he wrote, on occasion, moving prose that stands as literature in its own right.[7] "High technique", he wrote in the introduction to his first Year Book,

---

[1] *ibid.*, ii, 192.

[2] *H.E.L.*, ii, 31. Reference may be made to some of Maitland's more notable definitions in *H.E.L.*—chattel, ii, 32 and 116; felony, ii, 465; feud, i, 236 note; malice, ii, 468–469; owner, ii, 153 note; rent, ii, 129; seisin, ii, 29–31; serjeanty, i, 283; status (estate), i, 408. Note also on erroneous etymology, i, 294; on history of legal language, i, 80–87.

[3] 18 Oct. 1890, Maitland to Pollock, *Letters*, p. 86.

[4] *C.P.*, iii, 210–404.

[5] A. L. Smith, *Frederic William Maitland* (1908), p. 54.

[6] *Cambridge Law Journal*, i (1921), 297.

[7] e.g. *Year Books 1 &2 Edward II*, Selden Soc., vol. 17, pp. lxxx–lxxxi.

"is admirable whenever and wherever it is seen"[1]—and he had the subtlety of mind to appreciate, as well as the literary skill to celebrate, that technique. Sir Charles Ogilvie, indeed, accuses him of admiring it too much—to the detriment of equity's share in justice and the belittling of civil-law procedure.[2] Yet Maitland maintained a critical awareness of those points at which the common law was, or rather became, confused and inadequate. His first published article was a forthright demand for reform of real property law. In this paper, which appeared in the *Westminster Review* in 1879, he showed that he had no liking for medieval survivals for their own sake.[3] "We have never fairly cleared up that great medieval muddle which passes under the name of feudalism," he wrote twenty years later, "and until that be done, English Law cannot be stated in terms that would befit the modern code of a self-respecting nation."[4] Or again, copyhold tenure got short shrift from him. "The tenure still exists", he warned his law students, "a horrible nuisance as you will learn at large some day."[5] Nor did he readily submit to the tyranny of authority: he was especially, and repeatedly, critical of the great Sir Edward Coke.[6]

Returning to Maitland's significance for other sorts of history than the purely legal, we may make a negative point, which is that he was not a narrative historian. That his interests and inclinations leant towards a different sort of history is clear from the occasional comments he made on historians in the course of his correspondence. Gardiner he found hard to enjoy,[7] and in a letter to Fisher right at the end of his life, "Oman", he said,

[1] *ibid.*, p. xviii.

[2] Charles Ogilvie, *The King's Government and the Common Law* (1958), p. 31.

[3] *C.P.*, i, 195, "Was it necessary, we should not fear to maintain that no practical convenience, however small, is to be sacrificed on the altar of historic continuity."

[4] *C.P.*, iii, 438.

[5] *C.H.*, p. 50.

[6] e.g. *E.H.R.*, iii (1888), 570; *H.E.L.*, ii, 552 note, 563, 587 note; *The Mirror of Justices*, Selden Soc., vol. 7, p. ix.

[7] 22 Jan. 1900, Maitland to Sidgwick, *Letters*, p. 209.

"writes well but his is not the sort of history that I care for".[1] He himself had been asked to do the 1066–1215 volume in Longmans' *History of England*, but he had not accepted the invitation.[2] Only once amongst all his writings did he turn to narrative history—in his chapter on the Anglican Settlement and the Scottish Reformation in the *Cambridge Modern History*. Where his talent really lay was in a sort of descriptive analysis, characterized by a concreteness that led A. L. Smith to compare him to Macaulay.[3] More light-heartedly (and perhaps Maitland would have preferred it that way), his friend Leslie Stephen said that he sometimes feared Maitland had got permanently into the wrong century.[4]

Connected with his analytical power was his remarkable ability for formulating an historical issue or, in simpler terms, for asking the right questions. This Maitland regarded as one of the most important of the historian's functions: for instance, at the outset of *Domesday Book and Beyond* he said "some of the legal problems that are raised by it [Domesday Book], especially those which concern the time of King Edward, have hardly been stated, much less solved. It is with some hope of stating, with little hope of solving them that we begin this essay. If only we can ask the right questions we shall have done something for a good end."[5] Because he asked the right questions, Maitland greatly stimulated further study—not merely in general terms but along lines that he himself has specifically suggested. He did not, like his German professorial contemporaries, surround himself with research pupils, each with his assigned task within a framework of the professor's devising. He did not even, as his friend Vinogradoff was later to do in Oxford, develop the seminar system—though perhaps what the seminar was for Vinogradoff the Selden Society was for Maitland. Where Maitland's influence really lay, however, and indeed where it

---

[1] 12 Nov. 1906, Maitland to Fisher, *ibid.*, p. 383.
[2] 30 July 1901, Maitland to Poole, *ibid.*, p. 229.
[3] F. Smith, *Frederic William Maitland*, p. 8.
[4] 9 Apr. 1895, Stephen to Maitland, C.U. Add. MS. 7006.
[5] *D.B. & B.*, p. 2.

still lies, is through his books and the pointers to further investigation that they contain. This matter is particularly worthy of stress, because the later chapters of the present book will often concern theses of Maitland's that subsequent scholarship has caused to be abandoned and overturned. It is important not to leave the impression that this derogates from his greatness: on the contrary, it represents precisely the sort of progress in scientific historical inquiry that he envisaged and that his own work stimulated.

To reinforce what has been said about this aspect of Maitland's influence, it is worth while to give some examples of his pointing the path taken by subsequent scholars. It would not be unfair, for instance, to term Professor M. M. Postan's distinguished paper on the Chronology of Labour Services[1] as, in some sort, a gloss on Maitland's sentence in Domesday Book and Beyond, "We dare not represent the stream of economic history as flowing uninterruptedly from a system of labour services to a system of rents."[2] Or again, in a footnote to the same book, Maitland commented that the anatomy of Domesday Book deserved examination by an expert:[3] that was precisely what happened in 1953, and the findings of the experts who made the anatomical examination are reported in the official publication Domesday Re-Bound. Thirdly, Maitland's expressed wish that the broad features of Domesday Book should be set out in a series of statistical tables[4] is in process of realization in Professor H. C. Darby's Domesday geography studies.[5] So far our examples have been taken from Domesday Book and Beyond, but Maitland's other great books, and especially the History of English Law, supply comparable pointers that have been followed to advantage by half a century's historians. Such is his recognition of the lack of a separate concept of public law in medieval times,[6]

[1] T.R.H.S., 4th series, xx (1937), 169.
[2] D.B. & B., p. 58.
[3] ibid., p. 178 note.
[4] ibid., p. 407.
[5] ed. H. C. Darby, The Domesday Geography of England, i–iv.
[6] H.E.L., i, 230–231.

underlined and brilliantly illustrated by Professor T. F. T. Plucknett.[1] Because of the persistent influence that he has enjoyed in this sort of way, a study of Maitland brings us into contact with much of the most vital recent work on medieval English history.

So far we have not considered Maitland's literary presentation of his work, and yet as a characteristic of his achievement it was important. The fact that he not merely said good things, but said good things well, no doubt increased his influence on those who studied his writings. He never minimized difficulties or sought to oversimplify or to overclarify where some confusion was implicit in his sources. Only he tried, and rarely failed, to make what he was writing about sound interesting. His lucid, urbane style helped, and so did his wit. Of the high seriousness of his attitude there can be no doubt, and it would be a travesty to represent him as a joker. He was, however, the least pompous of men, with, as has been said, nothing of the *régent parcheminé* about him.[2] Each of his readers is entitled to his own private anthology of Maitland's witticisms: first place in my anthology of them would be filled by his description of the feudal system being introduced into England by Sir Henry Spelman and Sir Martin Wright,[3] and a close second what he had to say about the School of Pythagoras and that odd little triangle of ground behind St John's College, Cambridge, until recently owned by Merton College, Oxford, "endowed by its founder, by Walter Merton himself, with strips that he had purchased for reasons that I dare not guess".[4] Or again, in *Township and Borough* there is his charming distinction between *villa* and *villata*—"Whatever else Oxford may be, it is a *villa*, a town; and whatever else the community of Oxford may be, it is a *villata*, a township. A township should no more mean a little town than a fellowship should mean a little fellow!"[5] In only one connection did

---

[1] "The Lancastrian Constitution" in *Tudor Studies*, ed. R. W. Seton-Watson (1924); *Legislation of Edward I* (1949), pp. 75–76.

[2] G. Le Bras, "Le sens de la vie dans l'histoire du droit: l'oeuvre de F. W. Maitland", *Annales d'Histoire Economique et Sociale*, ii (1930), 390.

[3] *C.H.*, p. 142.   [4] *T. & B.*, p. 6.   [5] *ibid.*, p. 9.

Maitland perhaps overelaborate his witticisms—when they took the form of pseudo-pleadings or other semi-humorous adaptations of medieval common form.

Maitland's translations, too, were sometimes extremely witty. He rendered William of Drogheda's *cautelae* as "tips", "wrinkles", "dodges".[1] *Ivit domum pedibus et manibus* he translated "went home on all fours".[2] To the sentence in a deposition *Et dicit quod quidam parvus nuntius Willelmi Marescalli cum butonibus venit, etc.*, he appended the succinct footnote "Can this be an early appearance of the boy in buttons?"[3]

Reference to his translations serves to recall how very much of Maitland's working time was spent in editing records and other manuscripts. The techniques that he developed in that connection were marked by great common sense and a total absence of *mystik* and expertise for its own sake. At the outset of his career he had himself sat down, without palaeographical knowledge, and puzzled out his Gloucester roll of 1221, and he believed that others could do the same. He repeatedly made light of the difficulty of reading legal manuscripts—"anyone who knows some law and some Latin will find that the difficulty disappears in a few weeks".[4] He used to contend that in sixty hours spent over facsimiles he could turn out a man who would be able to read medieval documents with fluency and exactitude.[5] This recalls Stubbs's impatience with those who pleaded difficulty in reading charters—"Five minutes", he asserted with some exaggeration, "would suffice for mastering the writing if you would only take the trouble to apply your minds to it."[6] In these days of readerships in palaeography and of university diplomas in archives it is well to remember the common-sense contentions of these great practitioners.

Similarly, when it came to the presentation of documents in print, Maitland's attitude was eminently sensible. In his introductions to the various texts he edited he took care to make clear

---

[1] *R.C.L.*, p. 110.   [2] *Select Pleas of the Crown*, p. 58.
[3] *C.P.*, iii, 15.   [4] *ibid.*, ii, 60 note.
[5] *Sketch*, p. 171.
[6] W. H. Hutton, *Letters of William Stubbs*, Bishop of Oxford (1904), p. 282

the way in which he had worked. For instance, in the introduction to his first Year Book, "we shall, by the use of brackets," he wrote, "try to give the reader a fair opportunity of judging how defective is the editor's knowledge of old French and old law",[1] or, more succinctly, "Fidelity with a leaning to correctness should be our aim."[2] In adopting the method of extending medieval abbreviations he followed the preference of the old antiquaries Selden and Madox,[3] and rejected the use of special record type with which the Record Commission had experimented. "An appetite for abbreviated documents may come in time", he said in the introductory volume to *Bracton's Note Book*. "Even record type may be pronounced unsatisfying; readers will not be content until they can see the very upstrokes and downstrokes reproduced by photography; but to suppose that such an appetite exists at the present day, would be a foolish dream; to provide food for it, would be waste of money."[4] About the same date, too, he wrote along similar lines to Maxwell Lyte in connection with the scheme that had been mooted for republication of the old printed Year Books.[5]

Such, in general terms, were the principal characteristics of Maitland's work. A more detailed study of his achievement, it would seem, can best follow two different lines of inquiry. On the one hand, as it was admirably put by Professor G. Le Bras, "L'itinéraire scientifique de Maitland est, on le voit, compliqué. Les publications de textes alternent avec les études strictement personnelles et celles-ci portent sur des sujets dont le lien n'est pas toujours facile à discerner."[6] It would not be without interest, therefore, to follow Maitland's historical itinerary,

---

[1] *Year Books 1 & 2 Edward II*, Seldon Soc., vol. 17, p. lxxxiii.

[2] *ibid.*

[3] *Joannis Seldeni ad Fletam Dissertatio*, ed. D. Ogg (1925), p. 3; T. Madox, *Firma Burgi*, 1726, Preface.

[4] *B.N.B.*, i, 122. Note an acute palaeographical observation in *Year Books 3 Edward II*, Selden Soc., vol. 20, p. xiv—"Medieval stenography, it should be remembered, aimed rather at an economy of parchment than at an economy of time."

[5] 24 Apr. 1886, *Letters*, p. 17.

[6] *Annales d'Histoire Économique et Sociale*, ii, 390.

seeking to show how he came to move from one theme to another of his studies and what links existed between them in his mind: often we shall find that his correspondence gives us clues about this. On the other hand, it is desirable to attempt to evaluate Maitland's work within the separate areas in which he laboured, and in particular to set it in relationship to the specialized historical research of the half-century since his death. Both approaches are used in the chapters that follow.

II

DOMESDAY BOOK
AND PRE-CONQUEST HISTORY

THERE is an obvious convenience for the purpose of the present study in taking in chronological order the problems about which Maitland wrote, beginning with his Domesday and pre-Conquest writings. It is important to remember, however, that Maitland himself did not do this. His great edition of *Bracton's Note Book*, four or five volumes for the Selden Society, and above all the *History of English Law* all preceded *Domesday Book and Beyond*. At first sight it seems strange that this should be the case, for the time at which he commenced his career as an historian was one of great and fruitful activity in Domesday studies. It is true that, at that date, the official edition of the text of Domesday Book had already been in existence for a hundred years and the *General Introduction* by Henry Ellis for nearly three-quarters of a century. But what especially stimulated Domesday research was the appearance, in 1876, of the *Inquisitio Comitatus Cantabrigiensis* and the *Inquisitio Eliensis*, edited by N. E. S. A. Hamilton. In 1885 there were proposals for a Domesday Society, and, though the plan for this was not implemented, 1886 witnessed a week's Domesday commemoration meetings, arranged by the Royal Historical Society in co-operation with the Public Record Office and the British Museum: the papers read at these meetings were published in two volumes, the first at least of which contained material of importance. Yet ten years were to elapse before Maitland went into print on Domesday: there were various reasons for his delay.

The first of them need not detain us: it was simply one of those half-accidents that, in scholarship as in any other professional activity, seem to determine the course a man's careeer shall take. Maitland's first two major tasks in historical research had both concerned the legal records of the thirteenth century, and it is perhaps true that his most abiding interest was in the legal history of Angevin England. Certainly it was in that field that his work was most definitive.

As to more distant periods, though he felt the pull of early English history, he had never any illusions about its difficulty. "It would be foolish", he wrote later on in Stubbs's obituary, "to say that Dr Stubbs knew the earlier centuries as he knew the twelfth. That is impossible; the evidence is too small in quantity and too poor in quality. Many an investigator will leave his bones to bleach in that desert before it is adequately mapped."[1] This recognition of the difficulties of interpretation of pre-Conquest history led Maitland to approach them from the more certain ground of post-Conquest evidence, working backwards in time from the better to the less well known, as Seebohm had done in his *English Village Community*. The necessity for this sort of approach became for him, indeed, a constant pre-occupation. In 1887 he came near to warning his undergraduate class altogether off the ground of the Anglo-Saxon legal system: at a time when their Oxford contemporaries, the *Select Charters* in hand, were gaily advancing into that Serbonian bog, Maitland's pupils were advised of the need to "work backwards from the known to the unknown, from the certain to the uncertain".[2] The next year, in a review of T. E. Scrutton's *Commons and Common Fields*, he made precisely the same point, adding in his characteristically generous way, "Mr Seebohm was the first to see this, and whatever mistakes he may have made should readily be forgiven in consideration of this his great exploit."[3] More formally, on the serious occasion of his inaugural lecture as Downing Professor, he returned to the same theme. "If once we were certain of our twelfth century," he told his audience, "we might understand Domesday; if once we understood the state of England on the day when the Confessor was alive and dead, then we might turn with more hopes of success to the Anglo-Saxon

[1] *C.P.*, iii, 506.   [2] *C.H.*, p. 5.   [3] *E.H.R.*, iii (1888), 569.

dooms and land-books."[1] In a certain sense, then, this attitude of mind made his Domesday studies a by-product, albeit a very important one, of the *History of English Law*.

Yet, despite this ingrained attitude and the cautious approach that it involved, it is unlikely that Maitland would so long have resisted the temptation to publish on Domesday had there not been factors of a personal sort that made him hold his hand. One such was undoubtedly the reaction of Frederick Pollock, with whom, in 1889, he had entered into partnership to write the *History of English Law*. As early as the spring of 1891 Maitland told Bigelow that he was up to his eyes in Domesday,[2] and the term's lectures that he gave on it were written out in full.[3] His original intention was that what he wrote on Domesday, and especially about its implications for the history of Old English law, should form part of the joint *History*.[4] But Pollock, unwilling to raise so many hares, preferred a less-ambitious treatment of the pre-Conquest period: the chapter on Anglo-Saxon law, as he himself wrote it for the *History*, was short, thin, and indeed little more than introductory. As to Maitland's material, in the face of what he called Pollock's "agnosticism" he decided to put it on one side, "and leave D.B. [Domesday Book]", he told Vinogradoff, "to you and to Round".[5] That was in the summer of 1892, and though, two years later, he had a Domesday chapter for the *History* "in irretrievably printed sheets",[6] that, too, was a casualty. It is possible that Pollock may have been the cause of yet further delay, Maitland perhaps postponing publication of an independent article until Pollock's "Brief Survey of Domesday" should appear.[7]

It is fair to Pollock to add, however, that there were other influences of a personal sort that made for delay. "It is our misfortune", Maitland once wrote, "that, as we stumble through the

[1] *C.P.*, i, 482; for another example see *H.E.L.*, ii, 673.
[2] 19 Apr. 1891, *Letters*, p. 91.
[3] 10 Apr. 1892, Maitland to Round, *ibid.*, p. 100.
[4] 15 July 1895, Maitland to Poole, *ibid.*, p. 140.
[5] 29 May 1892, *ibid.*, p. 103.
[6] 15 July 1894, Maitland to Round, *ibid.*, p. 122.
[7] *E.H.R.*, xi (1896), 209.

night, we must needs stumble against some of our fellow adventurers",[1] and he seems to have become progressively more anxious not to get in the way of Vinogradoff and Round. With the former he had become intimate, helping him with the English edition of *Villeinage in England*; with the latter, a more complex and much more difficult character, his relationship was interesting.[2] At any rate, he kept both of them informed as to his plans, and his admiration for their work, added to his generosity, was yet another force for postponement. In the preface to *Feudal England* Round gratefully acknowledged Maitland's having withheld his conclusions until that work should have appeared.[3]

The publication of *Domesday Book and Beyond* finally took place in 1897, its actual title suggesting Maitland's adoption of Seebohm's technique and his intention of using the evidence of Domesday Book as a means of reaching back into the pre-Conquest period. This was possible because Domesday Book had been compiled in such a way as to show the changes that had taken place between the Confessor's death and its actual date of compilation, the *Tempore Regis Edwardi* entries making it as much a record of late Anglo-Saxon, as of Norman, England. As it was ultimately published, Maitland's book consisted of three long essays—the first on Domesday Book itself, the second on England before the Conquest, and the third on the Hide.

---

[1] *D.B. & B.*, p. 362.

[2] Miss Cam's account of the relationship (*Essays*, pp. xxiii–xxvii) cannot be bettered. Note also, *ibid.*, pp. 259–165, Maitland's *Athenaeum* review of Round's *Commune of London* (1899), to which Round took such exception that he broke off personal relationships. The only reference I should wish to add to those cited by Miss Cam is the characteristically generous statement by Maitland in 1901, after it had become abundantly clear that Round was utterly alienated, "His opinions are always weighty with me whether they agree with mine or not" (*C.P.*, iii, 143). In no connection was the contrast between Round and Maitland more marked than in their reaction to ill health: Round's chronic sickness goes far to account for his savage attacks on other historians, but Maitland's scholarly good manners were never affected by his poor health.

[3] *Feudal England* (1895), preface, p. 9.

In the first of the essays, and indeed in the very opening pages of his big book, Maitland gave a categorical answer to the problem of why Domesday Book was made. "One great purpose", he said, "seems to mould both its form and its substance; it is a geld book."[1] Or again, "Our record is no register of title, it is no feodary, it is no custumal, it is no rent roll; it is a tax book, a geld book."[2] This view Maitland shared with J. H. Round, and their thesis was not effectively challenged for almost half a century.

By Professor V. H. Galbraith, however, who has made himself the foremost Domesday scholar of our time, the theory has been vigorously assaulted. First in a long article, subsequently in one of his Ford lectures, and latterly in his monograph *The Making of Domesday Book*, Professor Galbraith has adduced weighty arguments against the geld-book theory.[3] He has insisted on the inherent improbability of the Conqueror concentrating so vast an administrative effort as was involved in Domesday upon the details of an annual custom, paid mainly by the lands of the unfree *villani*, when his far greater financial concern was with the manors of his own demesne and the honours of the great feudatories.[4] He has pointed out that the terms of reference of the commissioners who made the survey do not even mention the geld.[5] Most damaging of all to the geld-book theory, Professor Galbraith has argued that, as we have it today in its two volumes—Volume I for the greater part of England and Volume II in more detail for the counties of Essex, Norfolk and Suffolk—Domesday Book could certainly not be used as a geld book. Although a normal entry begins with the liability of an estate for geld, the volumes are organized within each shire according to fiefs—an arrangement that would have been useless for the assessment of the geld. "Geld was assessed", he puts it, "on the whole village, the payment being partitioned between

---

[1] *D.B. & B.*, p. 3.   [2] *ibid.*, p. 5.

[3] "The Making of Domesday Book", *E.H.R.*, lvii (1942); *Studies in the Public Records* (1948), ch. iv; *The Making of Domesday Book* (1961).

[4] *The Making of Domesday Book*, pp. 15–16.

[5] *ibid.*, p. 37.

the holders of the constituent manors composing it. In Domesday Book the various manors are widely separated under the fees of their holders, so much so, that it is not always possible, even by research, to find out the total geld obligation of the village. Thus . . . it is clearly absurd to describe Domesday Book (as Maitland does) as a 'geld book'. No wonder that elsewhere Maitland writes of the 'curious compromising plan of Domesday Book', which 'conceals' information given in the 'original returns'."[1] The reassessment of geld Professor Galbraith regards as a mere legend, a current dogma of the late Victorian age that Freeman passed on to Round, and Round to Maitland.[2]

An important part of the geld-book argument was that the original returns made by the Domesday commissioners, being on a geographical, not feudal, basis, were utilizable for geld assessment, and that only later were they codified into the two volumes of Domesday Book, then being set out in feudal form for different, and subsidiary, purposes. It is Professor Galbraith's especial merit to have shown this thesis to be untenable, neglecting as it does the evidence of the Exon Domesday and misinterpreting even that of the *Inquisitio Comitatus Cantabrigiensis* on which it was founded. His studies of the processes by which Domesday Book was made have sought to prove that the commissioners' returns from the various circuits were, in fact, in feudal form: that is, that they were organized in the same way as Domesday Book itself is organized, its first volume epitomizing, and its second volume virtually reproducing, them. If this argument is accepted—and it is cogently and impressively stated —then it makes it difficult to claim that, even in its earliest stage, the Domesday Survey was limited to the purpose of geld assessment.

As the debate stands at present, it would seem that the only remaining argument for the exponents of the geld-book theory is that the Conqueror intended, not merely a reassessment of geld, but a shifting of the basis of collection from the hundred to the fief, and that his death alone prevented experiment along

[1] *Studies in the Public Records*, pp. 96–97.
[2] *The Making of Domesday Book*, p. 26.

these lines.[1] But, however that may be, it takes us into the realm of the historical "if", and it is fair to admit that, when Maitland called Domesday a geld book, he meant something less vague than that, and that what he did mean was almost certainly wrong.

Should it, indeed, prove to be the opinion of those best qualified to judge that Professor Galbraith has demolished a central thesis of the first essay in *Domesday Book and Beyond*, there is nevertheless one connection in which it is possible to criticize what he has written. The point is one of historiography—almost, it might be said, of bibliography—and it concerns the relationship between Round's *Feudal England* and Maitland's book. For Professor Galbraith the latter is entirely derivative from the former. "Round's views", he says, "found favour with Vinogradoff; but their influence was most decisive upon F. W. Maitland. In *Domesday and Beyond*, published only two years after *Feudal England*, the views of Round were accepted and developed in a book of far wider appeal than Round's."[2] Elsewhere he even refers to Maitland as Round's "distinguished disciple".[3] This is surely to disregard the circumstances in which *Domesday Book and Beyond* had been written. It is true that, in his preface to that book, Maitland stated that, in the light of Round's work, he had "suppressed, corrected, added much".[4] But the same preface also explained that the greater part of what was in the book had originally been written for inclusion in the *History of English Law*[5]—that is, well before *Feudal England* appeared. The fact is that anyone writing within two years of the appearance of an important book of overlapping subject-matter finds himself in a difficulty with regard to his own, and his predecessor's, data. Maitland was no exception—"At a few points", he wrote to Round in September 1896, "I have doubted whether to repeat arguments that you have used or to take them for granted, and I am generally adopting the latter course,

---

[1] R. Weldon Finn, *The Domesday Inquest and the making of the Domesday Book* (1961), p. 31.

[2] *The Making of Domesday Book*, p. 13.

[3] *ibid.*, p. 15.

[4] *D.B. & B.*, preface, p. v.   [5] *ibid.*

saying 'this is proved, see Round, etc.' "[1] Superficially this may give an appearance of dependence on the earlier book, but, in fact, some of Maitland's footnotes[2] make it clear that many of his conclusions had been reached quite independently of Round. We know, moreover, from one of his letters to Poole that Maitland had made up his own mind on the importance of the *Inquisitio Comitatus Cantabrigiensis*.[3] That he was wrong in his adoption of the geld-book theory may well have been the case; but, if so, he was wrong, so to say, in his own right, and not because he followed and acted as a sort of popularizer of Round, as Professor Galbraith seems to think.

Maitland's preoccupation with the geld-book significance of Domesday led him to the adoption of a consequential theory about the manor: the geld, he thought, was the explanation of the great mass of manors recorded in Domesday Book. "A manor", he wrote in his famous definition, "is a house against which geld is charged"[4]—in other words the *manerium* of Domesday is not a manor in the thirteenth-century sense at all: it was not necessarily, in the east not even usually, coextensive with the vill. This highly technical definition of the *manerium* was at once queried by James Tait in his very important *E.H.R.* notice of *Domesday Book and Beyond*, in which he argued that the term was vaguer and less precise than Maitland believed.[5] He pointed out that, in pairs of entries concerning the same place in Domesday Book and the *Inquisitio Comitatus Cantabrigiensis*, the words *manerium* and *terra* appear to be used indiscriminately. Moreover, Maitland had admitted that a manor holden of another manor would, of course, be a damaging denial of the validity of his thesis,[6] and Tait was able to show that sub-manors of this kind were not such rarities as Maitland had believed. Tait was sceptical of the connection between *manerium* and geld: the vill, he held, was the real unit of taxation, and land was taxed where it physically lay even if it formed part of some distant

---

[1] 29 Sept. 1896, *Letters*, p. 151.
[2] e.g. *D.B. & B.*, 1 note, 11 note, 12 note, 121 note.
[3] 15 Aug. 1895, *Letters*, p. 168.   [4] *D.B. & B.*, p. 120.
[5] *E.H.R.*, xii (1897), 769–772.   [6] *D.B. & B.*, p. 128 note.

manor. That this criticism impressed Maitland is clear from a
letter he made haste to write to Tait. "I have never seen a review
of anything that I have written", he said, "which has taught me
so much or gone so straight to the points that are worth discussing. I cannot refrain from telling you of my gratitude . . .
I must confess that you have somewhat shaken one [of] my few
beliefs in the matter of the *manerium*, namely that this term had
some technical meaning. I can't give up that belief all at once,
but may have to do so by and by."[1]

Some further doubt was thrown on Maitland's belief by an
article of J. H. Round's which appeared some three years later.[2]
Although much of it simply developed Tait's arguments (without, incidentally, any mention of his review in which they had
been set out), nevertheless Round did cite pertinent examples of
berewicks gelding separately, and he posed the question—
awkward for Maitland's thesis—as to where the geld was due on
all those holdings in the *Inquisitio Comitatus Cantabrigiensis*
spoken of neither as manors nor as belonging to manors.

Most of all, of course, Maitland's definition of the *manerium*
suffers from the upsetting of the geld-book diagnosis of Domesday Book. Yet recent writers have been reluctant wholly to
abandon it. There must, after all, have been some specific legal
or fiscal meaning of the term *manerium* to have made worth
while the commissioners' patient effort to record manorial
status[3]—perhaps the latter rather than the former, "ease in collection, not legal responsibility", as Mr H. R. Loyn puts it.[4]

In the preface to *Domesday Book and Beyond* Maitland confessed
that, neither from himself nor from others, could he conceal
that he had in some sort been endeavouring to answer Seebohm,[5]
whose *English Village Community* had argued for a Roman
origin of the manor. The real point of Maitland's second essay,

---

[1] 20 Oct. 1897, *Letters*, p. 165.
[2] "The Domesday Manor", *E.H.R.*, xv (1900).
[3] Finn, *op. cit.*, p. 66.
[4] H. R. Loyn, *Anglo-Saxon England and the Norman Conquest* (1962), p. 339.
[5] *D.B. & B.*, preface, p. v.

especially, was to develop his own alternative thesis as to manorial origins, tracing what he regarded as the movement from freedom to dependence that he thought characterized English society between the seventh and the eleventh centuries. As he summarized his purpose, "We have been endeavouring to show that the legal, social and economic structure revealed to us in Domesday Book can be accounted for, even though we believe that in the seventh century there was in England a large mass of free landowning ceorls and that many villages were peopled at that time and at later times chiefly by free landowning ceorls and their slaves."[1]

This interpretation, independently reached by Vinogradoff, has held its own till the present day, and is indeed accepted by Sir Frank Stenton.[2] Recently, however, an acute paper by Mr T. H. Aston has queried the validity of the notion of a broad movement from freedom to dependence.[3] He points out, on the negative side, that much of the evidence for Maitland's thesis derives from a comparatively late date; that it is difficult to relate the free peasants of Domesday to the origins of English society; and that much of the structure of Maitland's argument is based on his belief, which Mr Aston does not share, that the landbooks transferred only a "superiority", an immunity, and not actual land.[4] Again, Mr Aston feels some doubt as to whether there is sufficient time between the supposed flourishing of a free peasant society, exemplified in seventh- and ninth-century laws, and the landlordship and manorialism of 1066, for the development to have taken place within that period. On the positive side, moreover, he suggests that Ine's laws of the late seventh century assume the existence of demesne and peasant land, characteristic of the manor; and that even behind Ine's laws, from the period directly after the Saxon settlement, the -ingas place names leave the impression that the earliest colonization was not organized differently from this later Wessex. Of

[1] ibid., pp. 326–327.
[2] Anglo-Saxon England, 2nd edn., p. 463 seq.
[3] "The Origins of the Manor in England", T.R.H.S., 5th series, viii (1958).
[4] D.B. & B., pp. 230–232.

course, Mr Aston's theory does not involve a return to Seebohm's belief in the Roman origins of the manor; but it does make those manorial origins earlier than Maitland thought and reduces the freedom that he believed the Anglo-Saxon peasant enjoyed in the age of the settlement and the period that immediately succeeded it. It is a forthright challenge to one of the central themes of *Domesday Book and Beyond*.

Reviewing Zinkeisen, *Die Anfange des Lehngerichtsbarkeit in England*, in 1894, Maitland suggested that the immunities granted by the Anglo-Saxon landbooks should be subjected to a thorough discussion.[1] That discussion he himself had the opportunity to provide in the course of the second essay in *Domesday Book and Beyond*, for he saw the alienation of jurisdictional rights from king to churches and thegns as another instrument for the subjection of the free peasantry. As a part of its movement into unfreedom, pre-Conquest society seemed to him to have suffered a marked growth of private, or seignorial, jurisdiction—that is, the exemption of wide areas from public, national justice. To this matter of the franchise, then, he gave extended treatment. What he wrote on the subject was subtly and attractively argued; but, more perhaps than anything else in his writing, it has received damaging criticisms, of such a nature, indeed, as to demolish the main structure of his argument.

The first of these criticisms, that of Professor J. Goebel, established that Maitland had exaggerated the extent to which actual jurisdictional functions were transferred.[2] Maitland himself was aware of the danger of confusing merely fiscal privileges with the delegation of jurisdiction. "We must be careful", he wrote, "not to introduce the seignorial court where it does not exist, and to remember that a lord may be entitled to receive the wites or fines incurred by his criminous men without holding a court for them."[3] Yet it was just this error, according to Goebel, into which he fell. Listing a group of Mercian and West Saxon charters of the period 767–888,[4] Maitland interpreted them

[1] *E.H.R.*, ix (1894), 600.
[2] Julius Goebel, *Felony and Misdemeanor* (1937), pp. 349 seq.
[3] *D.B. & B.*, p. 87.　　[4] *ibid.*, pp. 274–275, 282, 290–292.

as the earliest evidence of private court-keeping in England. This he did because the charters, exempting *ángild* out of the words of immunity, seemed to him to imply that, if a cause was between two men of the franchise, it was the lord's duty to see that the plaintiff was paid the *ángild*, while, should an action against one of his men be brought in a court outside the franchise, the lord might appear, pay the *ángild*, and thereupon obtain jurisdiction in his own court. What Maitland appears to have envisaged in either of these cases, then, was a transfer of the composition system from the royal to the franchise court,[1] and he made the *ángild* charters the foundation of his argument for the growth of private jurisdiction.[2] As Goebel pointed out, however, this argument was vitiated by being based on a false equation of *ángild* and *bot*. Actually, *ángild* is not composition at all, but simply restitution, and all that the *ángild* clause in the charters really does is to make the lord responsible for its payment as the ultimate security for his man.[3] Nor did Goebel accept that even grants of *infangtheof* involved more than a fiscal privilege.[4] Indeed, with a sweeping criticism, he claimed that none of Maitland's evidence really implied the transfer of judicial powers to the franchise holders.[5] If that negative case, stated in its extreme terms, is not proven, at least Goebel's arguments leave no doubt that Maitland both antedated and exaggerated the phenomenon of delegated jurisdiction.

Again, attacking on a narrower front than Professor Goebel, Miss Naomi Hurnard has effectively damaged the structure of Maitland's argument about seignorial justice.[6] The passage on which she sees the issue turn is Canute's Secular Dooms, chapters 12 and 15. Maitland assumed that the pleas listed in these chapters (*mundbryce, hamsocn, forsteal* and *fyrdwite* in Wessex; *fiht-wite, fyrdwite, grithbrice* and *hamsocn* in the Danelaw) represented the pleas of the crown and that everything outside them fell under grants of *sac* and *soc*—that is, that those lords who had

---

[1] Goebel, *op. cit.*, p. 352   [2] *ibid.*, p. 350.
[3] *ibid.*, pp. 351–353.
[4] *ibid.*, p. 367.   [5] *ibid.*, p. 374.
[6] "The Anglo-Norman Franchises", *E.H.R.* (1949), lxiv.

sac and *soc* had very wide jurisdictional powers indeed.[1] Miss Hurnard, however, has argued convincingly that the pleas listed do not represent the sum total of royal pleas, but should rather be thought of as marginal pleas: since *sac* and *soc* included some emendable causes, it was well to make clear which. The unemendable crimes were royal pleas, and these were not included in grants of *sac* and *soc*. If Miss Hurnard is right, as indeed she seems to be, then Maitland's picture of extensive private jurisdiction of the highest sort was notably exaggerated.

Finally, the scholar who has most of all made the medieval English franchise the field of her own distinguished scholarship, Miss Helen Cam, has added the weight of her authority to the criticism of Maitland's views.[2] Maitland clearly regarded the growth of seignorial jurisdiction as the result of the late Old English kings' irresponsible abandonment of the ruler's duties: he spoke of Edward the Confessor's granting away "large rights of justice",[3] even, "with reckless liberality", the reserved pleas of the crown.[4] This attitude Miss Cam has demonstrated, in some of her recent writings, to be unjustifiable. The alienation of royal power that Maitland imagined did not, in fact, take place. The mainly fiscal rights granted to certain great landowners were justified in that they gave them a monetary interest in putting down various sorts of violent crime;[5] but, in any case, in an age that still recognized private war the conception of crime as an offence against the state is scarcely relevant. The grants of pre-Conquest kings are a sign not of their weakness, but of their wisdom.[6]

In his second essay in *Domesday Book and Beyond* Maitland became involved in the further controversial question of whether feudalism had its roots in pre-Conquest England or was introduced by William the Conqueror—an issue as old as Spelman's

---

[1] *D.B. & B.*, p. 261.

[2] "The Evolution of the Medieval English Franchise", *Speculum*, xxxii (1957); "The Evolution of the Medieval English Franchise", *Schweizer Beiträge*, xv.

[3] *D.B. & B.*, p. 259.   [4] *ibid.*, pp. 282–283.

[5] *Speculum*, xxxii, 432.

[6] *Schweizer Beiträge*, xv, 174–175.

time and one that still divides historians today. His examination
of the land loans of the Bishop of Worcester (962–992), and
particularly of the memorandum in which St Oswald described
the terms in which they were made, led him to believe that they
bore the essential marks of feudalism. "Dependent tenure is
here," he claimed, "and, we may say, feudal tenure, and even
tenure by knight service."[1] As to how far general inferences
might be drawn from Oswaldslaw, it is true that he wrote
cautiously: but he clearly thought that they could.[2] This was to
take a view directly opposed to that advanced by J. H. Round
in perhaps his best-known essay—that knight service was introduced into England by the Conqueror and that Old English
practice had not anticipated it.[3] As between the two, historical
opinion has, until very recently, been heavily weighted in
Round's favour: Sir Frank Stenton, for instance, thought that
Maitland gave altogether too much precision to the very vague
language of Oswald's memorandum and that he attributed to
the bishop a far more constructive policy than its language
suggests.[4] On the other hand, work done in the last few years
has gone far towards redressing the balance in Maitland's favour.
Approaching the subject from very varied angles, and by no
means in agreement with each other as to all the details, recent
investigators do seem to have established the central facts that
military service in the pre-Conquest State was quite as specific
and as closely tied to land tenure as it was after 1066,[5] though,
of course, that is not to claim that by 1066 there had been much
progress towards the permanent hereditary land tenure, based

[1] *D.B. & B.*, p. 309.

[2] *ibid.*, p. 317.

[3] J. H. Round, *Feudal England*.

[4] F. M. Stenton, *The First Century of English Feudalism* (1932, 2nd ed.
1961), p. 124.

[5] E. John, *Land Tenure in Early England* (1961), ch. viii; M. Hollings, "The
Survival of the Five-Hide Unit in the Western Midlands", *E.H.R.*, lxiii
(1948); H. G. Richardson, and G. O. Sayles, *The Governance of Mediaeval
England from the Conquest to Magna Carta* (1963), ch. iii; C. Warren Hollister,
Anglo-Saxon Military Institutions (1962), esp. pp. 98–102, and "The Norman
Conquest and English Feudalism", *A.H.R.*, lxvi (1924–5).

on military service or its commutation, which had evolved by the late twelfth century.

"I am off to Horsepools," Maitland wrote to Poole on 20 June 1896, "in order that I may count hides in Domesday."[1] The third of the essays in *Domesday Book and Beyond* is a technical, statistical discussion of the problem of the hide, *hiwisc*, or *terra unius familiae*, an inescapable question Maitland thought, because on the size assigned to the hide turned so much of the interpretation of early English history. "In the construction of early English history", he said, "we shall adopt one style of architecture if we are supplied with small hides, while if our materials consist of big hides an entirely different 'plan and elevation' must be chosen."[2] The big hide of 120 acres, for which he came to argue, has, for instance, considerable importance in his thesis of the movement from freedom to dependence: it would be far too large a tenement for a serf or semi-servile *colonus*.[3] To the details of his case for the hide of 120 acres it is not possible to do justice within the scope of the present study. Two more or less incidental arguments may be noted, not so much for their intrinsic importance as because they are so typical of Maitland. The first he used when trying to explain away the very large assignments of hides to separate districts that are found in both Bede and the Tribal Hidage: in that connection he suggested an analogy with the governmental error of Edward III's reign when, for the purposes of the poll tax, it was estimated that there were 40,000 parishes in England instead of the 9,000 that did, in fact, exist.[4] The second he employed to meet the obvious criticism that a 120-acre hide appeared to be an over-large endowment of the *familia*—"Their fields of barley will be wide," he said almost flippantly, "for their thirst is unquenchable."[5]

Maitland's equation did not long pass unquestioned. An

1 *Letters*, p. 177.   2 *D.B. & B.*, p. 357.   3 *ibid.*, p. 361.
4 *ibid.*, p. 511.   5 *ibid.*, p. 519.

article of Tait's suggested a normal hide for central Wessex far smaller than 120 acres: he claimed that, for Wiltshire, 40 acres was the figure,[1] and, though that equation, too, has been upset, it is clear that the Wiltshire hide was small.[2] Moreover, Vinogradoff, confessing that the case did not look "so cheerfully simple" to him as Maitland had made out, commented very sensibly that if the relation of the hide to the actual occupation of the soil had been expressed on an average by the statement that it contained about 120 acres of arable, the elaborate inquiries of the Domesday commissioners about the number of plough teams would not have been necessary.[3] Indeed, the hide in Domesday Book has so many fiscal overtones that some historians have felt that the search for an acreage equivalent is pointless. Yet that it did bear a real relationship to area and value seems indubitable, though we still do not know what that relationship was.[4]

In 1900 Maitland admitted to R. L. Poole regarding *Domesday Book and Beyond*, "Of all that I have written that makes me most uncomfortable."[5] In the light of that admission, and of the successfully maintained criticisms of central, interlocking theses of the book, it may be wondered what is reckoned its permanent value and why a recent reissue[6] should have achieved a substantial sale. The simple explanation of both is, of course, that *Domesday Book and Beyond* is one of the great, fundamental books of English history.

Of its influence on subsequent scholarship some specific examples have been given on an earlier page,[7] and these might well be multiplied. Maitland's remark, for instance, that there is "no matter . . . darker than the constitution of the English army on the eve of its defeat"[8] was taken as a text, and a chal-

[1] *E.H.R.*, xvii (1902), 281.   [2] *V.C.H. Wilts*, ii, 182–183.

[3] *Growth of the Manor*, p. 157.

[4] R. Lennard, *Rural England 1086–1135* (1959), p. 341; Galbraith, *The Making of Domesday Book*, p. 48.

[5] 26 Aug. 1900, *Letters*, p. 217.

[6] Fontana edn., introd. Edward Miller, 1960.

[7] See above, pp. 12–13.   [8] *D.B. &B.*, p. 156.

lenge, by Mr R. Glover in his important paper on English Warfare in 1066.[1] Nor is it necessary to apologize on Maitland's behalf for those theses of *Domesday Book and Beyond*, basic though they are, that have been superseded. What has to be remembered is that he was doing something essentially new in early English historical scholarship, and that he had both to discover the facts and devise techniques for their interpretation almost while he wrote his book. "If we attack his position," perhaps the most distinguished of his critics has said, "it is with weapons that he himself has furnished."[2]

Moreover, apart from the detail of specific or technical influence, *Domesday Book and Beyond* and its author have had pervasive, personal effects that are not less real because they are hard to describe. One thinks of H. M. Chadwick, so different from Maitland in his approach, nevertheless recording in the preface to his *Studies on Anglo-Saxon Institutions* his special obligations to *Domesday Book and Beyond*,[3] or of Vinogradoff dedicating his *English Society in the Eleventh Century* to its author's memory, or, perhaps most of all, one recalls the story of G. T. Lapsley, many years after Maitland's death lunching with Professor Hazeltine in Downing College in the room that had been Maitland's study, and his emotional interjection, "Domesday Book stood *there*."[4] For over sixty years Maitland has been the master of those who wish to read early English history.

[1] *E.H.R.*, lxvii (1952).
[2] H. M. Cam, "The Medieval English Franchise", *Schweizer Beiträge*, xv, 172.
[3] *Studies on Anglo-Saxon Institutions* (1905), preface, p. viii.
[4] Powicke, *Modern Historians and the Study of History*, p. 130.

III

THE BOROUGH

MAITLAND's work on the history of the borough appeared in five places—Book II of the *History of English Law*;[1] a review article of Keutgen, *Untersuchungen über den Ursprung der deutsche Stadtverfassung*;[2] the first essay of *Domesday Book and Beyond*; his Ford Lectures, *Township and Borough*; and finally an introduction to Mary Bateson's and his *Charters of the Borough of Cambridge*. In this matter as in others he preferred to proceed from the relatively firm ground of the twelfth and thirteenth centuries backwards to the more debatable problems of pre-Conquest history. His chapter for the *History*, therefore, though it was the first of his borough studies to be published, was concerned with the later period. "The little that we can say of the Anglo-Saxon *burh* and the *burgess* of Domesday Book", he wrote in it, "will be better said elsewhere."[3]

It seems that, by 1895, Maitland was not merely turning his mind to the problem of borough origins but was feeling his way to his own highly controversial Garrison Theory. In that year, when Keutgen's important book appeared and came into Maitland's hands for review, it was its treatment of the military element in town development that most impressed him. "I believe this to be very important in the early English history", he told Poole,[4] and indeed the notice he wrote of Keutgen's study was at pains to point the moral for our own history. "To me it seems that we enter on a new and very hopeful line of

---

[1] See the second edition for his final views.
[2] *E.H.R.*, xi (1896), and *C.P.*, iii, 31–42.
[3] *H.E.L.*, 1st edn., i, 626.
[4] 15 July 1895, *Letters*, p. 164.

speculation", he said, "when we shift our attention from markets and handicraft and commerce to the military character of the ancient *burh*."[1] Certainly it was the importance of fortification and garrison that he came to stress most in his own writings on borough origins—his chapter in *Domesday Book and Beyond* in 1897 and *Township and Borough* the year following.

The problem that Maitland set himself to solve, it should be stressed, was one of legal history—what it was that brought about the differentiation of the borough from the ordinary vill. If he thought the first stage in the borough's legal history was represented by c. 40 of Alfred's Laws, where *burh* meant simply something that was enclosed, the crucial phase of development, as he saw it, came in Edward the Elder's reign with the Burghal Hidage.[2] This scheme, devised to ward off Danish attacks, whether made inland or from the coast, included thirty-one *burhs* in its main list, and assigned each of them—Maitland reckoned very significantly—a wide appurtenant area. So, he thought, came about the situation that he described succinctly in a famous sentence in *Township and Borough*—"The shire maintains the burh; the burh defends the shire."[3] He envisaged the tenth-century borough, then, as principally a fortress that was garrisoned by the shire thegns, who maintained in it *burgware* (warrior boroughmen) for its defence and the upkeep of its walls. For Maitland the *burgware* were the nucleus of the borough community and were determinant of the borough's development. It was to settle disputes between them that the king's peace was extended to the boroughs, from which there derived the independent jurisdiction of the *burgh-gemot* which, with the boroughs' special peace, later proved attractive to trade.[4] The *burgware*, too, Maitland thought were the ancestors of those burgesses recorded in Domesday Book as paying rent to manors outside the borough: in other words, their dependence on, and

---

[1] *C.P.*, iii, 38.

[2] *D.B. & B.*, pp. 183–184. For alternative views as to the date of the Burghal Hidage see J. Tait, *The Medieval English Borough* (1936), pp. 15–16.

[3] *T. & B.*, p. 37.   [4] *D.B. & B.*, pp. 190–192.

obligations to, external lords accounted for what he called the boroughs' tenurial heterogeneity,[1] which he reckoned was the basic cause of the later burgage tenure at a money rent that became so characteristic of the post-Conquest borough.[2] He thus argued that the two most notable features of the medieval borough—its court and its system of tenure—alike sprang from its military origins.

There were here two interlocking theses—one specific, that of tenurial heterogeneity, and one general, that of the whole Garrison Theory of borough origins. Both were vigorously attacked by James Tait, initially in his reviews of *Domesday Book and Beyond* and *Township and Borough*,[3] and forty years later in his book, *The Medieval English Borough*. Other critics also raised serious objections to both theses.

As to the first, the tenurial heterogeneity, supposed by Maitland to derive from the garrison obligations of the shire thegns of the period of the Danish invasions, in fact existed in Canterbury and Rochester in the eighth and ninth centuries.[4] Again, it is impossible to establish a regular proportion between the number of burgesses furnished by a manor and its extent—some had large numbers, and many, on the other hand, were exempt from the burden of maintenance.[5] Most difficult of all to explain away, the burgesses appendant to manors are rarest in just those Midland counties that Maitland thought most artificial and where the system might be expected to operate most completely.[6] Nor, where they are found, do they always belong to manors in the same shire as the borough.[7] An argument of Maitland's in favour of his tenurial heterogeneity thesis, not crucial to it but attractive, was also a casualty. He originally thought that *burh-geat-setl* (according to the available text of the eleventh-

---

[1] *ibid.*, pp. 189–190.   [2] *ibid.*, p. 198.

[3] *E.H.R.*, vii (1892), 772–777; xiv (1899), 344–345.

[4] *The Medieval English Borough*, p. 12.

[5] C. E. Petit-Dutaillis, *Studies and Notes Supplementary to Stubbs' Constitutional History* (1908), i, 81.

[6] *E.H.R.*, xiv (1899), 345.

[7] Petit-Dutaillis, *op. cit.*, i, 81.

century compilation, *Of People's Ranks and Law*, one of the qualifications of the ceorl "who throve to thegn-right") meant that he must possess a house in the *burh*; but his friend W. H. Stevenson was quick to point out that the omnibus word *burh-geat-setl* was a perversion, resulting from editorial tampering with the punctuation of the manuscript, that *burh-geat* and *setl* must be separated, and that the former meant no more than the possession of a manorial *burh*, some sort of mound or moat.[1]

These criticisms have weight, and Maitland's explanation of the causes of tenurial heterogeneity has not commended itself to historians. Yet two points must be made. First, if he erred, it was not, for the most part, through ignorance: he was not unaware, for instance, of the situation in eighth- and ninth-century Canterbury and Rochester,[2] nor of the failure of military and civil geography to correspond.[3] Second, if his explanation of the boroughs' tenurial heterogeneity is abandoned, as no doubt it should be, what is to be put in its place? As he himself wrote gaily, "What did the Anglo-Saxon thegn want with a town house? He was not going to spend 'the season' there in order that he might take his wife and daughters to the county balls."[4] Tait believed that rural landowners acquired property in the local town to secure a lodging for business visits or a refuge in time of war as well as because urban property seemed a good financial speculation;[5] Mary Bateson thought that the burgesses appurtenant to rural manors were simply country folk who, with a view to gain, had bought the freedom of the borough.[6] Yet neither notion seems a really satisfactory way of accounting for so widespread a phenomenon.

On the greater matter of the Garrison Theory in general, Tait's criticisms were certainly effective. If the primary basis of the borough constitution was, indeed, military, then, as he said, "why do we never hear of a burh-gerefa"?[7] And is it not

---

[1] *D.B. & B.*, p. 190; Stevenson, *E.H.R.*, xii (1897), 489–492; *T. & B.*, pp. 209–210.

[2] *D.B. & B.*, p. 182.   [3] *ibid.*, p. 189 note.   [4] *C.P.*, iii, 38.

[5] *The Medieval English Borough*, p. 31.

[6] *E.H.R.*, xx (1905), 149.   [7] *E.H.R.*, xii, 774.

strange that the tenth and eleventh centuries, a stormy enough
period, should see Maitland's *burgware* turning into solid bour-
geois citizens?[1] It is generally held today that most of the
English *burhs* of the period of the Danish wars were basically
different in kind from Henry the Fowler's artificial boroughs,
created some years later against the Magyar threat to Germany.
Most often they were rather the fortification of existing settle-
ments than new creations, and the foundation of a *burh* at
Worcester was accompanied by the grant of a market.[2] It was,
indeed, the matter of trade as an influence on borough origins
that most of all gave an edge to Tait's critical reaction to the
Garrison Theory. He felt that Maitland seriously underrated the
effect of the commercial factor in early borough development.
In this connection, Carl Stephenson came strongly to Maitland's
defence: the argument of his *Borough and Town* was that it was
only after the Norman Conquest that the boroughs became
significant mercantile centres. Stephenson's interpretation, however, has not been generally accepted.

Maitland himself was more inclined to admit the validity of
Tait's criticism. He wrote to him on the appearance of the
review of *Domesday Book and Beyond*, "If ever I have to make a
second edition of that book I shall have to alter many things in
it in the light of your criticisms. Certainly this would be the
case in the matter of the boroughs",[3] and the year following,
in the appendix to *Township and Borough*, he admitted that
certain important towns, notably Norwich, did not fit the
Garrison Theory.[4] In the light of Tait's reviews he recast his
borough chapter for the second edition of the *History of English
Law*, and what he came to believe on the difficult subject of
origins may be found there as follows:

> For at least a century and a half before the Norman Conquest,
> English law has known the borough as something different from
> the ordinary *tún* or vill. The typical borough has been (i) the *burh*,

[1] *ibid.*, 775.

[2] D. J. V. Fisher, "Economic Institutions in the Towns of Medieval
England", *La Ville, Deuxième Partie* (Rec. de la Société Jean Bodin, 1955),
p. 533.

[3] 20 Oct. 1897, *Letters*, p. 165.   [4] *T. & B.*, p. 210.

(ii) the *port,* and (iii) the moot-stow of a shire. (i) It has been a fast-ness and place of refuge whose earth-works have, at least in some cases, been maintained by the men of the shire. It may even have been in some sort a garrison town: the great people of the shire may have been bound to keep in it houses or "haws", as they were called, and "knights" of the old English kind. (ii) A market has been held in it: that is to say, it has been one of the few places in which men might buy cattle and other goods without putting their necks in jeopardy; their bargains were attested by official witnesses and toll was taken from them. (iii) It has been the meeting-place, the moot-stow of the shire, and perhaps because it was the county's town, it was in no hundred, but had a court of its own, a burh-moot or port-moot, which was co-ordinate with the hundred-moots. Moreover, a severe and exalted peace, the king's *burhgrið,* had reigned within it.[1]

This represented a substantial cutting down of his earlier thesis. It may be that originally Maitland had let himself be too much influenced by Keutgen, and perhaps we may even turn against him one of his own sentences—"Explorations in foreign climes may often tell us what to look for, but never what to find."[2]

Some of the most vivid and attractive pages in Maitland's writing are those in the first lecture of *Township and Borough,* where he reminds us that "those who would study the early history of our towns . . . have fields and pastures on their hands".[3] In that volume he included Loggan's print of the open fields of Cambridge, and the agrarian element in the medieval and post-medieval period is something that he stressed through-out the lectures. Even in Oxford, which had remarkably little arable land, and where the manors of Holywell and Walton came right up to the north wall of the town, Maitland thought that these manors had been formed out of an earlier, more agricultural Oxford. In his review of *Township and Borough,* Tait commented on Maitland's increased stress on the borough's agrarian substructure, and probably intended to convey that he was in some danger of exaggerating it. Certainly, when, much later, he was replying to Stephenson, Tait argued that it was possible to overstress the importance of fields and pastures, even

---

[1] *H.E.L.,* i, 636–637.   [2] *T. & B.,* p. 24.   [3] *ibid.,* p. 9.

for the eleventh-century borough. The "eating away of burghal arable", as he termed it, had begun first around the old Roman cities, and by 1066 much borough land had come into the hands of both lay and ecclesiastical magnates.[1] It is fair to add, however, that Tait's strictures were directed at Stephenson and not at Maitland. Maitland, indeed, had taken care not to press his claims too far: he noted that in the time of Edward the Confessor Cambridge was gelded at 100 hides, that is, paid about ten times the normal Cambridgeshire village, from which he drew the conclusion that "its taxable wealth did not lie wholly in its fields".[2]

When he turned his attention to the post-Conquest borough the core of the problem remained the same for Maitland—how did the borough come to be differentiated, and distinguished, from the ordinary vill? He thought that this resulted from a kind of conspiracy between the king and the borough to squeeze out all save royal lordship—something that could be done because of the weakness of the lords consequent upon tenurial hetero-geneity. "As time goes on", he put it, "the burgesses, who are coalescing in a new type of community, will be treated as a unit which has no lord but the king, and will pay tallages when the king's demesne manors are tallaged: but they will make their profit of their communal 'immediacy' by depriving all land-lordship of its lordly character and reducing it to the level of a mere right to rent."[3] This may be a correct diagnosis of what happened, but it does not explain why it occurred, and there is perhaps substance in Carl Stephenson's complaint that Maitland failed to appreciate the revolutionary effect on the borough of commercial development, even if that development was earlier, and longer-term in its operation, than Stephenson himself was prepared to admit.[4] It was the boroughs' financial potentialities and the king's financial difficulties that secured their privileges.

As a legal concept, the borough of Edward I's time was a place endowed with various franchises. For his chapter in the

[1] *The Medieval English Borough*, pp. 68–77.
[2] *T. & B.*, p. 50.   [3] *H.E.L.*, i, 638.
[4] *Borough and Town*, p. 138 note.

History of English Law Maitland listed nine categories of these, granted piecemeal in the twelfth and thirteenth centuries—jurisdictional privileges, tenurial privileges, mercantile privileges, the *Firma Burgi*, property of the borough, election of officers and government of the borough, by-laws and self-government, self-taxing powers, and the Gild Merchant.[1] The brilliant sketch in which he outlined the development of each of these privileges was basic to subsequent historical work on the borough. It provided the pattern for Ballard's *British Borough Charters 1042–1216* and its two continuation volumes,[2] Ballard stressing that his aim was to discover the steps in the development of each burgensic privilege and to demonstrate which of them were common and which exceptional, seeing this as the way in which a definition of the borough might ultimately be formulated.[3] Of course, the material in *British Borough Charters*, as well as that in Mary Bateson's *Borough Customs*,[4] made it possible for borough historians to expand what Maitland wrote in the last decade of the nineteenth century; so, on the crucial matter of the *Firma Burgi*, did the extensive publication of the early pipe rolls.[5] Nevertheless, in general terms Maitland's account of the post-Conquest borough has stood up well to the work that has been done since he wrote it.

In 1891, when he reviewed Gross, *The Gild Merchant*, Maitland had asked, "Will the day ever come when the boroughs of England will print their records?"[6] As was so frequently the case when he wrote in that vein, he himself was later to take what action he could towards an affirmative and constructive answer to the question he had raised. In 1901 he published with Mary Bateson *The Charters of the Borough of Cambridge*, and in the introduction he wrote for that book he was able to reiterate

[1] *H.E.L.*, i, 643–669.

[2] A. Ballard and J. Tait, *British Borough Charters 1042–1307* (3 vols., 1913–23); M. Weinbaum, *British Borough Charters 1307–1660* (1943).

[3] *British Borough Charters 1042–1316*, p. xiv.

[4] Selden Society, 1904 and 1906. Maitland read this in manuscript, in slip, and in page. "Good fortune it was." (*C.P.*, iii, 542.)

[5] Tait, *The Medieval English Borough*, pp. 139–193.

[6] *C.P.*, ii, 231.

M.–D

his point about the gradual build-up of borough franchises in a different, and curiously effective, way—simply by a straight-forward, chronological examination of the successive Cambridge charters. The introduction, indeed, forms an interesting comple-ment to his sketch of borough privileges for the *History of English Law*.

If all this side of Maitland's borough studies reveals his talent for descriptive analysis at its best, the borough history to which he had become so deeply committed also brought into play his ability to deal with abstract ideas. With reference to the second edition of the *History of English Law* which he was preparing, he wrote to Round in 1898, "I shall be glad of early intelligence if anything about fee farms and bailiffs is on the point of appearing, for a much renovated chapter on the boroughs will be the last part of my 'history' that will go to press."[1] This renovation had, in his view, become necessary because of two separate factors—on the one hand, as we have seen, he thought it well to say something more of the Garrison Theory and of other matters of borough origin; on the other, he had been studying Gierke, *Genossenschaftsrecht*, which encouraged that interest in the prob-lem of the corporation that was to loom so large for the rest of his life. Important parts of both that chapter and of *Township and Borough* were concerned with the development of corporateness.

This was the sort of question involving the interaction of theory, on the one hand, and hard economic and political facts on the other, which especially appealed to Maitland. A formal theory of the corporate body as *persona ficta*, he demonstrated, was slow in emerging and, when it did so, derived from the thirteenth-century canonists, notably Pope Innocent IV. In some degree the facts had preceded the theory, and before the end of the thirteenth century the organization of at any rate the greater boroughs was such as to demand a new idea.[2] Even on the factual side, however, development, he thought, was slow and partial. The franchises that the boroughs had purchased from the crown had been bought by the subscriptions of some of the

[1] 22 Mar. 1898, *Letters*, p. 173.
[2] *H.E.L.*, i, 687.

burgesses, and some definition of who was to enjoy these franchises no doubt became necessary. Yet though this meant that,
in practice, some features of incorporation appeared, Maitland
warned against antedating modern ideas of the essence of corporateness, stressing the slow emergence in the medieval borough
of the contrast between *its* and *ours*. That distinction could hardly
come about until the borough had at its disposal a revenue over
and above the fee-farm rent that it owed to the crown: "A
'corporate personality' is hardly required until there is a corporate
income."[1]

One element in borough development that was of importance
in the growth of corporateness Maitland tended to underrate, or
at least he made its appearance slower and more gradual than
perhaps it really was. That was the council. It was his view that
the council grew naturally out of the borough court, and he
did not see it—generally at any rate—exercising administrative
and judicial functions earlier than the fourteenth century. When
fuller information became available, however, Tait was able to
build up a formidable mass of evidence for councils of earlier
date, and these he insisted were not a derivation from the old
borough court but a consciously created new municipal organ.
The association of the council, in its earliest years, with the
office of mayor suggested to him that they were the product of
the communal spirit of the last decade of the twelfth, and the
early years of the thirteenth, centuries.[2] May they not have owed
something to French influences—more than Maitland allowed?
He did introduce, as a sort of saver, in his chapter in the *History
of English Law* an admission that, in the movement towards corporateness, "the influence of the sworn *communa* of the French
town may be suspected",[3] and some years later, reviewing
Round's *Commune of London*, "Assuredly we must keep our
eyes on France", he wrote.[4] But it is true that he scarcely seems

---

[1] *T. & B.*, p. 205.
[2] *The Medieval English Borough*, pp. 263–301, especially pp. 286–289.
[3] *H.E.L.*, i, 671.
[4] *Essays*, p. 263.

to have realized the full extent of the influence of the French communal movement.

One other aspect of Maitland's borough work must be mentioned: his *Township and Borough* is a fine, and very charming, piece of local history. Delivered in Oxford as the second series of Ford Lectures, it was based on a close and affectionate observation of the Cambridge where Maitland taught. "Will you think me ill bred", he asked his audience, "if I talk of the town in which I live?"[1] He seems, indeed, to have been led to publish the actual lectures less for their own sake than as preliminary generalizations to the long appendix on Cambridge which he placed after them. "I want you to do for me a really brotherly act," he wrote to Fisher on 3 December 1897, "and to tell me from the bottom of your heart whether those lectures to which you were kind enough to listen are worth print. I have got stuff for a book about the Cambridge Field and this I am minded to publish in any case. My thought had been to make the stuff an appendix to my lectures; but now I am hesitating. Every one at Oxford was enormously kind, but just for this reason I feel sadly in need of a little objective criticism . . . Treat me as a brother on this occasion."[2]

In the upshot, of course, for every one reader of the appendix to *Township and Borough* there have no doubt been a hundred readers of the lectures that form its text. All the same, the appendix has importance as an acute piece of very detailed topographical scholarship, and most of its learning still stands after half a century's active antiquarian investigation of the problems of Cambridge history. The editor of the *Place-Names of Cambridgeshire and the Isle of Ely* prefers to derive Landgrytheslane, the ancient lane that became the modern Pembroke Street, rather from a "long stream" than from Maitland's "limit of the ordinary land-peace".[3] Miss Cam has printed corrections to his list of mayors of Cambridge.[4] But Carl Stephenson's rash attack

[1] *T. & B.*, pp. 3–4.
[2] 3 Dec. 1897, Maitland to Fisher, *Letters*, pp. 165–166.
[3] P. H. Reaney, *Place-Names of Cambridgeshire and Isle of Ely* (1943), p. 47.
[4] *V.C.H. Camb.*, iii, 38.

on Maitland's argument for the early existence of Cambridge south of the Cam failed utterly.[1]

The local element in Maitland's borough studies is in some ways reminiscent of his friend Cunningham's use of Cambridge evidence in the *Growth of English Industry and Commerce*.[2] The achievement of both in this connection seems worth stressing, when it is remembered that their work was done before the *Victoria County History* and its editors began to devise modern techniques of local historical scholarship. But apart from technique, both enjoyed the advantage, not always possessed by *Victoria County History* authors, of an intimate knowledge of their area, acquired by living in it over the years. Perhaps there ought to be a residence qualification for local historians. However that may be, for anyone who was educated and spent his early, impressionable years at Cambridge, *Township and Borough* has the greatest charm of all Maitland's writings. Such a one, perhaps, could not feel marked enthusiasm when, a few years ago, Cambridge was created a city. It is true that there are medieval precedents for its being termed a *civitas*; but for some of us Maitland made it the borough *par excellence*. It was singularly appropriate that, on New Year's Day 1900, the council of the Borough of Cambridge made him a freeman of the borough.

[1] Carl Stephenson, *Borough and Town* (1933), pp. 200–202; Cam, *Liberties and Communities in Medieval England* (1944), pp. 1–18.

[2] A. Cunningham, *William Cunningham* (1950), p. 57.

IV

THE HISTORY OF ENGLISH LAW TO 1272: PREPARATORY AND BACKGROUND STUDIES

MAITLAND's most effective work, the part of his writings that has best stood up to half a century's subsequent scholarship, was in the legal history of Norman and Angevin England. The basis of his great learning in this field was the research he undertook in the four or five years prior to his election as Downing Professor—work that bore immediate fruit in two books, *The Pleas of the Crown for the County of Gloucester, 1221*, which he published in 1884, and *Bracton's Note Book*, which appeared three years later. Without the knowledge he gained in preparing these two publications—and especially the latter—he could never have produced the monumental *History of English Law*.

Of the two early books the first is, of course, infinitely the less important: except for two or three short articles, it was Maitland's earliest work in legal history, and it perhaps remains his least known. Yet apart from its interest as the work of his apprentice hand, it has genuine value on its own merits. The text is a transcription of that part of the record of the Gloucestershire eyre of 1221 which relates to the pleas of the crown, and as such gives a detailed picture of the working of the thirteenth-century criminal law. The introduction, a mere forty pages, is an excellent essay of generalizations based on, and interpreting, the text. It includes what is still perhaps the best, as it is certainly the most interesting, sketch of the working of the thirteenth-century criminal law—the *murdrum* and Englishry, frankpledge, amercements and proof (by appeal, ordeal and, just beginning to make its appearance for this purpose, a tentative use of the jury.)[1] For human interest Maitland was fortunate inasmuch as Engelard de Cigony and others of the barons' *bêtes noires*, proscribed in chapter 50 of Magna Carta, had been active in the county in John's reign, and the evidence of the cases he had edited gave him the opportunity of discussing the activities of this important group.[2] Finally, his introduction shows that same touch of familiarity with, and love for, the area with which he was concerned that we have already noticed in his later work, *Township and Borough*. As early as 1866 he had inherited Horsepools, a Gloucestershire manor-house, from his grandfather, S. R. Maitland, and his text took him over familiar ground—

> if it be but luck that sends us to Gloucester, still the lot has fallen to us in a fair ground. There is less need to speak of place than of time. The year 1221 is gone for ever, the county of Gloucester is where it always was, and hardly a name of village or hamlet is mentioned in this roll that cannot be found, perhaps a little clipped and twisted, on the modern ordnance map. Still we may just note that the great shire which joins Warwick to Somerset, and Berks to Monmouth, is a good specimen county. There is land of every kind, the Cotswolds, the Severn Valley, the wild forest of Dean, while, in the thirteenth century, there was hardly a county with two such towns as Gloucester and Bristol.[3]

"A good specimen county" was what Maitland claimed for the Gloucester of his text; yet inevitably, limited as it was to a single county, *The Pleas of the Crown for the County of Gloucester, 1221* bore some similarity to the archaeologist's experimental trench across his site or to the sociologist's random sample approach to his data. It is therefore worth mentioning that Lady Stenton in three large Selden Society volumes, by transcribing most of the remaining eyre rolls of the first five years of Henry III's reign, has in some sense completed the task that Maitland's slim volume began.[4]

[1] See, however, the interesting comments in T. F. T. Plucknett, *Edward I and Criminal Law* (1960), pp. 72–76.

[2] *Pleas of the Crown for the County of Gloucester, 1221* (1884), pp. xiii–xcii.

[3] *ibid.*, p. xix.

[4] Selden Soc., vols. 53, 56 and 59. Mr C. A. F. Meekings has kindly

His Gloucester volume was scarcely through the press before Maitland turned his attention to *Bracton's Note Book*. To Vinogradoff belonged the credit of recognizing the probability that B.M. Add. MS. 12269 was a collection made by Bracton and used by him in compiling his *Treatise*.[1] This discovery he conveyed to Maitland in their famous conversation in the Parks at Oxford on 11 May 1884 and to the learned world in general in a letter of 19 July 1884 to the *Athenaeum*. Maitland's credit is to have followed up this pointer and to have produced in 1887 his great three-volume edition of the *Note Book*, with an invaluable first volume of apparatus and introductory matter in which he established beyond reasonable doubt, not only the relationship of the *Note Book* and the *Treatise*, but also of the *Note Book* and the plea rolls from which its cases were copied. These two modest scholars later exchanged typically generous letters about the apportionment of credit between them. "I have been able to add a few links to the chain of argument that you forged", Maitland wrote to Vinogradoff.[2] "You have done everything in your power to show off any little merit I may have had in the case" was Vinogradoff's comment to Maitland.[3]

Maitland undertook the publication at his own cost, as he tells in the preface in one of the most charming apologies ever made by an author—"I have often had to count the cost; also to reflect that another day in the Record Office or the British Museum would mean another hundred miles in the train . . . Perhaps I was not the man for the work; but I have liked it well."[4] He dedicated the book to Henry Sidgwick, by whom,

informed me that still unpublished are the civil pleas roll of the 1219 Devon eyre (P.R.O., J.I. 1/180) and the fragmentary survivals of the 1221 Hereford eyre (P.R.O., J.I. 1/300 A).

[1] G. E. Woodbine argues that "Tractatus" must have reference to the treatise on actions, not to the whole book (Bracton, *De Legibus et Consuetudinibus Angliae*, ed. G. E. Woodbine (1915 et seq.), i, 37). In this chapter, however, "Treatise" is used as a term to describe the whole of Bracton's book.

[2] 12 June 1887, *Letters*, p. 32.

[3] Nov. 1887, Vinogradoff to Maitland, C.U. Add. MS. 7006.

[4] *B.N.B.*, i, p. ix.

as already mentioned, he had been taught for the Moral Sciences Tripos at Cambridge and who had founded the readership which he held. From some of his surviving papers we know that he presented copies to Stubbs, to the American legal historian, Bigelow, to Edward Fry, to Alfred Wills, and because, no doubt, of its local topographical interest, to Exeter Cathedral Library. One other recipient must, for a particular reason, be mentioned —Maitland gave a copy of the *Note Book* to Coleridge, the Lord Chief Justice, and, with a rare flash of pride, endorsed Coleridge's acknowledgment "from the Right Honourable the Lord Chief Justice of England".[1] Nor is this list of those who received presentation copies complete: Maitland no doubt made gifts from the publisher's stock of the book as occasion arose—for instance, the copy in the Library of New College, Oxford, bears his inscription to Edward Jenks.

Maitland's edition of *Bracton's Note Book* had a twofold significance—first for the light it shed on the career of Bracton himself and on his *Treatise*, and second for the stimulus given by this splendid collection of cases to the detailed study, by Maitland and others, of thirteenth-century law. The present chapter deals mainly with the former topic.

Henry of Bracton was born *c.* 1200. Alternative claims have been made for two Devonshire villages, Bratton Fleming and Bratton Clovelly, as his birthplace; the issue between the two was not settled by Maitland, but Round later showed that Bracton held a knight's fee of Baldwin le Fleming and had other connections with the Fleming family, so that the evidence is in favour of the former.[2] Bracton was, of course, in the line of succession of the great judges of the first half of the thirteenth century who had so large a share in the making of the medieval common law— Simon of Pateshull, Martin of Pateshull and William Raleigh. Maitland suggested that Raleigh was perhaps Martin of Pateshull's clerk,[3] and, if so, he would get into his hands the plea rolls that Bracton (in turn Raleigh's clerk) was later to use; Sir

---

[1] C.U. Add. MS. 7006.

[2] Round, "Bractoniana", *E.H.R.*, xxxi (1916).

[3] *Pleas of the Crown for the County of Gloucester*, 1221, p. xiii.

Cyril Flower went farther and claimed that the first five of Pateshull's surviving rolls were substantially written by Raleigh.[1] This latter view has been questioned and must perhaps be regarded as not proven;[2] still, it is inherently probable that these men learnt their law by the characteristically medieval method of apprenticeship, each beginning his career by serving as clerk to his predecessor. From 1245 on to 1267 Bracton served as a justice in eyre, especially in his own West Country; he also acted in the same period as a justice *coram rege*, but it was in the south-west that his main work was done. About his connections in that part of England and the names of places and people that crop up in the *Note Book* Maitland had an attractive and highly typical passage—

> Even in imagination it is pleasant to walk in Devon. We take the train to Barnstaple; Bracton was archdeacon of Barnstaple. The next morning we may stroll easily to Raleigh, the cradle of the great house, and so on through Heanton Punchardon and Braunton Gorges to Saunton, the manor which Bracton held . . . the way lies straight across Dartmoor; it is a wild way but (teste meipso) there is none pleasanter in England . . . Many questions are solved by walking; Beati omnes qui ambulant.[3]

Bracton's treatise, the *De Legibus et Consuetudinibus Angliae*, based as it was on a wide experience, both direct and vicarious, of thirteenth-century law, Maitland bracketed with Blackstone's *Commentaries* as the greatest of English law books. "Twice in the history of England", he claimed, "has an Englishman had the motive, the courage, the power to write a great, readable, reasonable book about English law as a whole."[4] About its date of composition there is some doubt. Maitland thought that the main part was written between 1250 and 1258 and that this was added to by Bracton down to the date of his death—that is, the whole treatise, according to him, is the work of Bracton the judge, not Bracton the clerk of William Raleigh. Kantorowicz,

---

[1] *Curia Regis Rolls*, viii, p. vi.

[2] C. A. F. Meekings, "Martin Pateshull and William Raleigh", *B.I.H.R.*, xxvi (1953).

[3] *B.N.B.*, i, 103.   [4] *ibid.*, p. 8.

in his *Bractonian Problems*, argued for an earlier date. He tried to show that William of Drogheda, an Oxford jurist who wrote a practical book on procedure in ecclesiastical courts, knew Bracton's text and, since William was killed in his house at some time before 1245, that this implied an earlier date for the *Treatise* —that it was, in fact, the work of Bracton the clerk rather than of Bracton the judge.[1] Mr Richardson, however, has countered this argument effectively:[2] the influence, he thinks, was the other way round (that is, it was Bracton who knew William's work) and, since the *Treatise* contains a copy of the chapters of the Eyre not in the version of 1244 and reference to the king's return from Gascony in 1254, he comes down in favour of Maitland's dating.[3]

However it may be over the question of date, there is no doubt that the principal significance of the *Treatise* was its bringing together the custom applied by Bracton's immediate predecessors as judges. Already by his time what we should today call judge-made law was a characteristic of the English legal system. As Bracton put it himself, "Si autem aliqua nova et inconsueta emerserint, et quae prius non fuerint usitata in regno, si tamen similia evenerint per simile judicentur."[4] This, of course, is not to say that Bracton held the view that a more recent judgment was preferable to a previous one, still less that he would have understood the modern implications of *stare decisis*.[5] All the same, he clearly believed that much of English law depended on decided cases and in the course of the *Treatise* cited nearly five hundred cases, most of them heard before Martin of Pateshull or William Raleigh. What Vinogradoff noticed, and Maitland proved beyond all reasonable doubt, is that the *Note Book* was a preliminary collection of cases extracted from the plea rolls by clerks working under Bracton's guidance and that he ultimately used them for citation in the *Treatise*. Of the close on fifty pages of tightly reasoned argument by which

---

[1] *Bractonian Problems* (1941), pp. 27–36.
[2] "Azo, Drogheda, and Bracton", *E.H.R.*, lix (1944).
[3] See also Cam, *Studies in the Hundred Rolls* (1921), pp. 23, 89.
[4] Bk I, c. 2.   [5] *H.E.L.*, i, 209.

Maitland established this relationship between the *Note Book* and the *Treatise* we must content ourselves with quoting his final summary of the evidence—

> Our two writers not only select the same rolls, rolls of Pateshull and Raleigh, ponder over the same cases, hold the same juristic theories, use the same unusual phrases, but also are interested in the same counties, in the same set of people, Arundells, Punchardons, Traceys, Raleighs; they have personal as well as professional interests in common.[1]

To this he added that both made the same mistake over the baronial *Nolumus* of 1234, and passed to his wittily phrased conclusion—

> Must we not say then that, until evidence be produced on the other side, Bracton is entitled to a judgment, a possessory judgment? *Et ideo consideratum est quod Henricus recuperauit seisinam suam, saluo iure cuiuslibet.*[2]

Nor was it only the relationship forward from the *Note Book* to the *Treatise* that Maitland was able to demonstrate: he also traced many of the *Note Book* cases back to the plea rolls, where they were marked in the margin in all probability by Bracton himself.[3] It may be true, as Lady Stenton has maintained, that Maitland exaggerated the difficulty of finding the originals of Bracton's citations.[4] Certainly the same writer's suggestion that the *Note Book* once contained cases from a number of other assize rolls is interesting: it is based on the fact that, though none of the marked cases in her two rolls turns up in the *Note Book*, reference to some of them is made in the *Treatise*.[5] These, however, are refinements, and refinements of a scholar who has been generous in her admission of indebtedness to Maitland's edition of the *Note Book*.

The rationalization of English law at an early period by

---

[1] B.N.B., i, 104.   [2] *ibid.*, p. 107.   [3] *ibid.*, pp. 66–69.

[4] *Rolls of the Justices in Eyre for Yorkshire*, 1218–19, Selden Soc., vol. 56, p. xii.

[5] *Rolls of the Justices in Eyre for Lincolnshire*, 1218–19 *and Worcestershire*, 1221, Selden Soc., vol. 53, p. xi.

Bracton was no doubt, as Maitland thought, one of the factors that in subsequent centuries saved England from a Reception of Roman law. But another factor that made the common law tough enough to withstand a formal Reception was that through Bracton it did receive something of Romanist principles. In this connection Maitland almost certainly thought too little of Bracton. Seven years after the appearance of the *Note Book*, he published his *Bracton and Azo* with the comparable pieces of the two texts printed in parallel, and his conclusion from this exercise was that the Romanist element in the *Treatise* was not very considerable—not a thirtieth part came from the *Corpus Juris* and perhaps only a fifteenth from Azo; and what there was he found frequently corrupt and imperfectly understood. "He is an able man," he wrote of Bracton, "but he is a poor, an uninstructed Romanist."[1] Other scholars have thought this judgment unduly severe, and they have sought explanations of the odd errors in Bracton's citations of Roman law other than his own ignorance of it. Even Kantorowicz's invention of a "haplographical redactor" amongst the copyists of the *Treatise* to account for these errors, fantastic though it seems at first sight,[2] has commanded a wide range of support, though there is not agreement as to whether this irresponsible copyist worked after Bracton's death or was possibly his clerk, working during his lifetime.[3] If this haplographical havoc remains hypothetical (and McIlwain's objection that it was odd for a copyist, so alert when copying English law, always to go to sleep when he turned to Roman does seem to have weight),[4] there are many occasions where Bracton's divergence from Azo or the Digest is attributable neither to his, nor a copyist's, error, but to the sources that he used. Nearly a hundred years ago Twiss showed that Bracton's discussion of homicide was influenced by Bernard of Pavia;[5]

[1] *Bracton and Azo*, p. xviii.   [2] *Bractonian Problems*, p. 41.
[3] Plucknett, *Early English Legal Literature* (1958), p. 56.
[4] C. H. McIlwain, "The Present Status of the Problem of the Bracton Text", *Harvard Law Review*, lvii, 229.
[5] *Henrici de Bracton de Legibus et Consuetudinibus Angliae Libri Quinque* (Rolls Series), ii, p. lix.

Maitland in his turn indicated that his doctrine of putative marriages was borrowed from Tancred's *Summa de Sponsalibus et Matrimonio*, a canon of the Fourth Lateran Council, and a decretal of Alexander III;[1] and Vinogradoff stressed his use of collections of extracts, especially of Vacarius's *Liber Pauperum*.[2] What the last-named argued was that the divergences were partly due to Bracton's use of second-hand source material, and partly, too, to his effort to interpret Roman, in the light of English, law.[2]

This rehabilitation of Bracton as a Romanist, and the fact that opinion has turned against Maitland in this connection, perhaps raises the question of how good a Romanist Maitland himself was. Certainly he lacked formal, academic training in the Roman law; certainly he himself spoke slightingly of his own competence in it, confessing that he had acquired "the very little, the almost nothing" that he knew of it late in life in order to understand some sides of English history,[3] and telling Poole that his *Bracton and Azo* was "a work of ultra-trepidation, for I don't know any Roman law and consequently I should like to hear whether I have been guilty of many 'howlers'."[4] But before these considerations are taken too seriously, it is necessary to remember two things. First, a great deal of Maitland's best work was done in areas where he was, and indeed had to be, self-taught—and we do know that he began, though he did not complete, a translation of Savigny's *Geschichte des Romischen Rechts*.[5] Second, his almost pathological modesty has to be taken into account: Maitland's ignorance was most times a good deal more learned than other men's scholarship. What is true, however, is that he did not know—and we still do not know—enough of the influence of the early glossators in England. At any rate, whatever may be the truth regarding Bracton's understanding of Roman law and Maitland's assessment of it, Maitland at least understood that Bracton's ventures into Roman law did have an important effect on his legal thinking. This, after

---

[1] *Bracton and Azo*, pp. 221–224. [2] *Collected Papers*, p. 239.
[3] *Bracton and Azo*, p. xxxiii. [4] 15 July 1895, *Letters*, p. 165.
[5] W. S. Holdsworth, *The Historians of Anglo-American Law* (1927), p. 132.

all, is the crucial point—far more important that the transplantation of this or that legal device.[1] Without the new attitude, the common law might well have proved inadequate for the needs of the developing English state.

A final point about Maitland's Bractonian studies may also be discussed. In the course of preparing his edition of the *Note Book*, he quickly became aware of the complete inadequacy of Twiss's edition of the *Treatise*, which had appeared in the Rolls Series in 1878–1883. "I live in constant fear", he wrote to Bigelow as early as 1885, "that some German or Russian or even Turk will edit Bracton and shame the nation which produced certain six volumes of rubbish (innuendo etc.)."[2] More than most men he was familiar with the *Treatise*, and especially with the Digby MS. 222 of it in the Bodleian Library, to which, indeed, he kept returning. On 5 February 1893 he wrote to Fisher that he wished to come to Oxford to see it again—"My knowledge of Oxford inns is limited to the chill splendour of the Randolph and I should like, if this may be, to find a homelier place."[3] Or again, to the same correspondent he wrote on 24 June 1895, "I want to spend one day in the Bodleian with my old friend the Bracton MS."[4] The same year he expressed the hope in print that the day was not very far distant when the Selden Society would be able to put in hand an edition of Bracton, the foundation of which he thought would be the Digby MS. Yet he understood that the editor's work would be long and should not be undertaken in haste.[5]

To the task of editing the *Treatise*, of course, Maitland himself never got round, and for this the world of legal scholarship had to wait till Professor Woodbine's edition of 1915–1940. Woodbine, it may be noted, did not accept the especial primacy and importance attached by Maitland to the Digby MS.; he found no reason to believe that it was made immediately from Bracton's

[1] Plucknett, *Edward I and the Criminal Law*, p. 6.
[2] 31 Oct. 1885, *Letters*, p. 16.
[3] Bod., F. P., Box 27.
[4] Bod., F. P., Box 27.
[5] *Bracton and Azo*, p. 250.

own copy.[1] Nor did he agree with Maitland's division of the *Treatise*, with c. 9 marking the point at which Bracton turned from Roman to pure English law: this seemed to him to be quite simply not the case, since almost from the start sections that are thoroughly English follow sections of Roman derivation.[2] Yet in spite of these fundamental differences of opinion, and though he had never known Maitland personally, Woodbine acknowledged that in the plan of his edition Maitland's influence was at least as great as that of any other one person.[3]

As was said earlier in this chapter, the work that Maitland did on *Bracton's Note Book* had a double significance—for Bracton in particular and the history of thirteenth-century law in general. It was the second rather than the first of these that was to attract Maitland most. The *Note Book* was, as Lady Stenton has put it, "a great mass of cases which served the authors of the great *History of English Law* as a quarry from which they could draw much of their raw material for the account of legal development in the age of Bracton".[4] Maitland's achievement in that connection is the subject of the next chapter.

Before turning to that topic, however, we have one other element in Maitland's preparatory studies that is worth consideration. Amongst the lectures that he gave after his return to Cambridge in 1883 and before his election to the Downing Professorship five years later was a course on English constitutional history. Though only published posthumously—they appeared in 1908, edited by his brother-in-law, H. A. L. Fisher —these lectures, under the title *The Constitutional History of England*, became Maitland's most widely read book, reprinted twelve times between 1909 and 1955, and in 1961 appearing in a paper-back edition. Some of his most enthusiastic followers, notably Miss Helen Cam, have found reason for regret that he should be best known for this early, general and untypical work, dependent mainly on secondary sources and lacking the original

---

[1] Bracton, *De Legibus et Consuetudinibus Angliae*, ed. Woodbine, i, 77.

[2] *ibid.*, p. 38.   [3] *ibid.*, p. x.

[4] *Rolls of the Justices in Eyre for Lincolnshire 1218–19 and Worcestershire, 1221*, Selden Soc., vol. 53, p. vii.

scholarship of his later books.[1] It is probable that Maitland would have agreed with them, for, as Fisher tells us in his preface to the *Constitutional History*, its author remarked, "I have written a course of lectures in six months on Constitutional History. Do I publish it? No."[2] Yet generations of students in the history schools of British and American universities would have been the poorer for the lack of this volume. Moreover, apart from its absolute value, the *Constitutional History* had some significance as a background to Maitland's subsequent studies in legal history. First and foremost, it represented a preliminary clearing of the ground, a necessary familiarization with the printed sources before its author could pass profitably to his own original work. Second, it must be remembered that the lectures were given to men reading for the Law Tripos, which ensured that they should have a strong legal slant, and so the first quarter of the *Constitutional History* was a preliminary survey of much of the ground Maitland later examined in detail, while the remainder of the book—what Tout would have called "a great sweep through history"—gave him an invaluable framework within which to set his later studies. Again, the whole arrangement of the book is very unusual and personal; it is interesting just as any great historian's views on history of a more general kind are bound always to be interesting. The influence of the *Constitutional History* was not, of course, so direct or so basic to Maitland's work as a legal historian as was that of *Bracton's Note Book*. All the same, it would be wrong to think of these lectures as simply the fulfilment of a teaching obligation peripheral to their author's real interests. They are an integral part of his developing scholarship.

[1] *Essays*, p. ix.
[2] *C.H.*, p. v.

V

THE HISTORY OF ENGLISH LAW TO 1272: DEFINITIVE WORK

WHILE *Bracton's Note Book* was in the press Mr Edward Dove of Lincoln's Inn circularized the Inns of court with notice of a meeting to consider the establishment of a society to encourage the study of English legal history. The detailed story of the Selden Society's origins is yet to be written;[1] but at such time as it is it will become apparent just how much the society owed to Maitland. His was one of the names of members of the Bar attached to the preliminary notice as supporters of the proposal; he served on both council and executive committee of the society; he edited four out of the first eight of its annual volumes, wrote an introduction to a fifth, and throughout the remaining years of his life read in proof every page of every volume issued.[2] Also in those later years he inaugurated the society's Year Book series, undertaking three volumes on his own and a fourth jointly with G. J. Turner. If these last demand separate treatment,[3] about his publications in the society's first decade something must here be said, because they form an integral and important part of his work on the legal history of Angevin England.

In the memoir that he wrote of Maitland, H. A. L. Fisher described his strategy for the newly founded Selden Society as being to exhibit rapidly the range of its operations. "It was better", said Fisher, "to begin upon several different types of

[1] See, however, Holdsworth, "The Jubilee of the Selden Society", *L.Q.R.*, lv (1939).

[2] *Year Books 3 & 4 Edward II*, Selden Soc., vol. 22, p. x.

[3] Below, ch. VII.

record than to work one vein without intermission."[1] If that was true of Maitland's choice of material and subject-matter for the society's annual volumes, it was also true of what he did internally within the volumes that he himself edited. So it was that the first volume to make its appearance, the *Select Pleas of the Crown*, published in 1888, consisted of extracts of early thirteenth-century pleas alike before the justices in eyre, the Bench, and the king himself. This gave a sufficiently wide range of record material to enable Maitland to generalize valuably in his introduction, where he traced the gradual differentiation in the *curia regis* that was taking place in the period. The volume was able to serve as a pointer and a programme-maker for the publication of the early records of the royal courts. When it was published little of this material was in print apart from the Record Commission's *Abbreviatio Placitorum* and Palgrave's *Rotuli Curiae Regis*; but the *Select Pleas of the Crown* has had distinguished successors.[2] Incidentally it is worth mentioning that one of the earliest of them, the Pipe Roll Society's *Rolls of the King's Court*, 1194–5, though not transcribed by Maitland, had an introduction by him which contained a useful description of the actions available in the last decade of the twelfth century.[3]

It was characteristic of Maitland's effervescent productivity that the society's first volume was not off his hands before his mind was turning to a similar selection of manorial pleas. "I know no rolls more interesting than the earliest manorial rolls"; he told Ames in January 1888, "they are covered with litigation; I hope that the Selden Society will soon make a selection from them."[4] The Selden Society in this context, of course, meant Maitland himself, and it is no surprise to find him writing to Vinogradoff a mere nine months later that his introduction to the manorial rolls was taking shape:[5] presumably

---

[1] *Sketch*, p. 54.

[2] There is a list of early printed plea rolls in *Select Cases of Procedure without Writ under Henry III*, Selden Soc., vol. 60, pp. xi–xii.

[3] Pipe Roll Soc., xiv, pp. xxxii–xxxvii.

[4] 30 Jan. 1888, Maitland to J. B. Ames, *Letters*, p. 37.

[5] 14 Oct. 1888, *Letters*, p. 49.

the transcription of Latin records that were to occupy over a hundred and fifty pages of print, and possibly their translation, too, had been accomplished in the meantime. The *Select Pleas in Manorial Courts* appeared in 1889, and like the earlier volume contained selections from the records of different, and contrasting, jurisdictions. It consisted of rolls of the ordinary manor courts of the abbots of Bec, Ramsey and Battle, and of the abbess of Romsey; of the abbot of Ramsey's honorial court of Broughton; of his manor court of King's Ripton, which was on the ancient demesne; of his fair court of St Ives; and of the abbess of Romsey's hundred court of Whorwelsdown. As well as separate introductory notes to each of these, Maitland provided what he termed an "overgrown" general introduction to the volume: the most important sections of this were perhaps his sketch of the means by which the royal courts came to usurp the lord's jurisdiction over free tenants[1] and his carefully argued rejection of Coke's thesis which required that every manor should have at least two freehold tenants.[2]

It was originally Maitland's intention to produce a second volume of manorial pleas,[3] but, in fact, this idea was not implemented. Instead, two years later he published, with W. P. Baildon, *The Court Baron*—four texts of tracts on the holding of feudal courts and a record of late thirteenth- and early fourteenth-century pleas in the Bishop of Ely's court at Littleport. The introductions to these were briefer, and of less general significance, than that of the previous volume. The truth was that, with the Selden Society launched, in these years Maitland suffered from an *embarras de richesses*. "I wish that I were allowed to make *three* Selden books this year", he wrote in a letter of 1888.[4]

His fourth volume for the society, *Bracton and Azo*, was a work of very different kind, and has already been mentioned.[5] What is worth a word in the present context, however, is his

---

[1] *Select Pleas in Manorial Courts*, Selden Soc., vol. 2, pp. lii–lx.
[2] *ibid.*, pp. lx–lxxiii.
[3] The title-page describes the book as Volume 1.
[4] [Sept.] 1888, Maitland to Vinogradoff, *Letters*, p. 49.
[5] Above, p. 53.

introduction to W. J. Whittaker's edition of *The Mirror of Justices*, which Coke, with his "uncritical voracity",[1] had believed to be a genuine collection of Anglo-Saxon law. Maitland's essay is a wholly delightful piece of academic gaiety, though his tentative conclusion as to the authorship of the *Mirror*—that it was the *jeu d'esprit* of a young layman, perhaps Andrew Horn, has not passed unchallenged.[2]

Maitland's inaugural lecture as Downing Professor of the Laws of England, which he delivered in the autumn of 1888, and to which he gave the promising title, "Why the History of English Law is not written",[3] was, it must be confessed, disappointingly negative. There were perhaps two reasons why the lecture was not more successful. First, it is clear from a letter that he wrote to Vinogradoff just after he had delivered the lecture—he speaks of "getting through" it—that he was far from well at the time.[4] Second, there is point in Professor Plucknett's alternative title, "Why the Selden Society cannot find editors".[5] About Maitland's own productivity for the society something has been said above, but the other side of that medal was the difficulty in securing other editors, and the slowness with which the interest of English scholars was aroused worried him much in these early years. A letter that he wrote to Bigelow in the summer of 1888 shows the sort of anxiety on these counts that he was feeling.[6] However that may be, the inaugural lecture's pinning of hope on the historical activities of briefless barristers was, for Maitland, quite extraordinarily unrealistic, and, to quote Professor Plucknett again, "His later career saw the gradual abandonment of the propositions laid down in 1888."[7] Perhaps it was that he became more and more

[1] *The Mirror of Justices*, Selden Soc., vol. 7, p. ix.

[2] Review by F. Pollock, *L.Q.R.*, xi (1895), 393; J. S. Leadam, "The Authorship of the Mirror of Justices", *L.Q.R.*, xiii (1897); H. G. Reuschlein, "Who wrote the Mirror of Justices?" *L.Q.R.*, lviii (1942); N. Denholm-Young, *Collected Medieval Papers*, p. 79.

[3] *C.P.*, i.

[4] 14 Oct. 1888, *Letters*, p. 49.

[5] Plucknett, *Early English Legal Literature*, p. 11.

[6] See above, pp. 7–8.   [7] *op. cit.*, p. 13.

an historian as time passed, though the converse proposition that
he became less a lawyer would certainly not be true.

The Selden Society had included in its original outline of
objects the collection of materials for a history of English law,
but that soon became the joint commitment of Maitland and
Sir Frederick Pollock, and eventually virtually the commitment
of Maitland alone. "Pollock and I have mapped out a big work,
too big I fear for the residue of our joint lives", he told Bigelow
on 24 November 1889,[1] and a little less than five years later
Pollock was reporting to Mr Justice Holmes, "Maitland and I
have a whole volume of history in type."[2]

It is one of the supreme oddities of bibliographical history
that, through the mere accident of Pollock's seniority to Maitland at the Bar, we should know as Pollock and Maitland a book
that, as to well over nine-tenths, Maitland wrote. "I want to
tell you how little of the *History of English Law* is my writing",
Pollock confessed to Holmes, going on to admit that it amounted
to the chapter on Anglo-Saxon law and the bulk of the early
history of contract.[3] This seems to make inadequate his post-
script to the preface of the first edition—"It is proper for me to
add for myself that, although the book was planned in common
and has been revised by both of us, by far the greater share of the
execution belongs to Mr Maitland, both as to the actual writing
and as to the detailed research which was constantly required."
On this J. H. Round commented with characteristically tart
effectiveness, "F.P.'s caveat was quite needless. The hand of
Esau was lesss distinctive than the pen of the Downing Professor."[4]
Some years later, when, in 1903, the Swiney Foundation prize,
consisting of a sum of money and a silver cup, was conferred on
the authors of the *History of English Law*, the *Oxford Magazine*,
discussing the equitable division of the prize, suggested that "the
Bart might keep the cup". Actually, the division agreed upon
seems to have given Pollock a fifth of the cash payment, and
there is evidence that the takings of the book had been divided

[1] *Letters*, p. 75.   [2] *Pollock-Holmes Letters*, i, 52.
[3] *ibid.*, i, 60–61.
[4] 28 Mar. 1895, Round to Maitland, CU. Add. MS. 7006.

on this basis.[1] If that was indeed the case, Pollock may be regarded as having been fortunate financially no less than in
reputation.

Perhaps the matter of Pollock's collaboration with Maitland
may fairly be put in stronger terms than that, for there is some
evidence that suggests that his influence on the book came
dangerously near to being adverse. Maitland, the most patient
and loyal of men, admitted to Vinogradoff, who was entirely in his
confidence, that he did not much like the Anglo-Saxon chapter
which was Pollock's main contribution. At Pollock's insistence
he had cut out his own Domesday material,[2] but he felt that his
collaborator's chapter, which replaced it, though shorter in
treatment, nevertheless made difficult the inclusion of anything
about Old English law in the later part of the *History*. He went
on to tell Vinogradoff quite frankly that he was pressing on with
the Norman and Angevin periods so that Pollock might have
little to do before the time of the Year Books.[3] Basically the
two men were thinking in different terms and planning their
book on different scales. As early as October 1890 Maitland had
written a most revealing letter to Pollock—

> And now I want to speak about the size of our book. I go on
> writing and writing, for I have so arranged my lectures that I have
> little else to do. Thus matter accumulates at a great rate. I know that
> some of it deals with rather minute points; but the more I see of
> cents XII and XIII the more convinced am I that their legal history
> must be written afresh with full proof of every point . . . So you
> see the person that you have to deal with, and if you decide to
> dissolve partnership I shall not be in a position to complain of the
> decision. I quite see that a brief history of English law is much
> wanted and might be written, but I also see that I can not write it.
> Every day my admiration for Stubbs grows, and you know what
> this form of worship condemns one to.[4]

In the light of this letter, can one doubt that Pollock had been

[1] *Letters,* pp. 137–139.
[2] Above, p. 19.
[3] 29 May 1892, Maitland to Vinogradoff, *Letters,* p. 103.
[4] 18 Oct. 1890, *ibid.,* p. 86.

agitating for a less comprehensive, and very much less significant, book than the *History of English Law* proved to be?[1]

Incidentally, it is amusing to note that, apart from his own
great book, Maitland was influential in bringing about the
expansion of Holdsworth's *History of English Law*. That had
originally been commissioned as a "short history", but there is
an extract of a letter of Holdsworth's in which he told Maitland
that, on his advice, he was extending it to three volumes.[2]
Eventually, of course, it ran to fourteen.

The Pollock and Maitland *History* was published in 1895. It
was well received,[3] and within three years went into a second,
revised edition, which is generally used for scholarly purposes
and citation today.[4] Turning to its content, it is difficult to know
where to begin—or, for that matter, where to finish—discussion
of a work that stands along with Bracton and Blackstone as a
great classic of English law. All that will be attempted in the
present context is to describe, in the most summary and outline
fashion, the *History's* plan, to indicate some of its most influential
theses, to draw attention to the points at which they have been

[1] If the evidence permitted it, a study of Maitland's relationship with
Pollock would be interesting. They had known each other from the late
'seventies, when both were members of Leslie Stephen's Sunday Tramps: in
1883 one of Maitland's wittiest letters conveyed his congratulations to Pollock
on his election to the chair of Jurisprudence in Oxford (Sir John Pollock,
Time's Chariot, p. 59). In one of the tributes that he wrote on Maitland's
death (*Quarterly Review*, April 1907) Pollock spoke of him with great warmth
and claimed that he and Maitland were "fast friends and allies". So, in a
sense, they were. But the two men were of widely different temperament, and
Pollock's character not wholly sympathetic—"That a screen did surround his
qualities", his son admits, "is undeniable" (*op. cit.*, p. 48). Maitland was too
gentle to reveal any adverse reaction to Pollock even in private correspondence,
though he did tell his friend Jackson in 1903 that he thought Vinogradoff
would make a better professor of Jurisprudence at Oxford than either Pollock
or Maine (13 Dec. 1903, Maitland to Jackson, *Letters*, pp. 288–289). Mrs
Maitland, with less inhibitions in the matter, wrote to Bigelow in 1897, "I
fear Sir F. Pollock meditates a visit to us very soon. I know you will sympathise
with me for this" (*Boston University Law Review*, xxxvii, 310).

[2] 5 Nov. 1906, C.U. Add. MS. 7008.

[3] Notices by E. Fry, *E.H.R.*, x (1895); Bigelow, *A.H.R.*, i (1895).

[4] Second edition 1898; reprinted 1911, 1923, 1952.

modified by subsequent scholarship, and finally to attempt an appreciation of Maitland's technique.

The *History of English Law* was divided into two Books—not, of course, to be confused with the two volumes in which it was published. In the first of these, the "Sketch of Early English Legal History", the approach was chronological. For this sort of account of the early medieval history of English law the authors were fortunately placed, for they were heirs to the material made available in the course of the nineteenth century by the Record Commission, the Rolls Series, the Camden and Surtees Societies, and more lately by Liebermann and the Pipe Roll and Selden Societies.[1] They had, too, amongst secondary works, the stimulating example, in the matter of constitutional history, of Stubbs. What is especially notable in this first Book, however, is the striking capacity that Maitland showed for organizing and presenting the data that had been brought within his reach. This kind of general survey was, as a matter of fact, something at which he was especially good, as he had shown, eight years before the publication of the *History of English Law*, in his lectures on Constitutional History,[2] and was to show again in the article on the history of English law that he contributed to the *Encyclopaedia Britannica*—written at Las Palmas, it was termed by its author "work of a bookless imagination".[3] Moreover, alongside this neatness and clarity of exposition Maitland possessed the ability to highlight a significant development in a succinct sentence or to phrase a crucial question in an unforgettable way.[4] The first Book is the most generally studied portion

[1] *H.E.L.*, i, p. xxxv.   [2] They were only published posthumously, however.
[3] [4 Dec. 1889], Maitland to Pollock, *Letters*, p. 204.
[4] e.g. discussing the relationship in the late twelfth century between the royal courts and the canon law, "Henry's greatest, his most lasting triumph in the legal field was this, that he made the prelates of the church his justices" (*H.E.L.*, i, 132); or seeking a definition of feudalism, "Shall we say that French feudalism reached its zenith under Louis d'Outre-Mer or under Saint Louis, that William of Normandy introduced feudalism into England or saved England from feudalism, that Bracton is the greatest of English feudists or that he never misses an opportunity of showing a strong anti-feudal bias?" (*H.E.L.*, i, 67).

of the *History of English Law*: Miss Cam has gone so far as to call it "indispensable reading for anyone who would understand the origins of our constitution".[1]

The second, and much longer, Book, entitled "The Doctrines of English Law in the early Middle Ages", set out the rules of law in the period 1154–1272, and was analytical in method. It opened with four important pages in which Maitland described the arrangement of its chapters and the reasons for that arrangement.[2] Land tenure, he thought, should be dealt with first because it was basic to the law on its public side, and from tenure the transition was natural to personal condition and to the law of jurisdiction and the communities of the land—closely connected as these were with the land law. Only after these matters had been handled did Maitland think it right to turn to the more private branches of the law—ownership and possession; contract; inheritance; family law; crime and tort; procedure. The scheme was logical; and if it involved, as any scheme must, some repetition, Maitland used this with skill to underline his central theses.

For Maitland the fundamental feature of the medieval English land law was the bold simplicity of its central concept,[3] and with a statement of that concept he opened his discussion of tenure:

> Every acre of English soil and every proprietary right therein have been brought within the compass of a single formula, which might be expressed thus: *Z tenet terram illam de . . . domino Rege.* The king himself holds land which is in every sense his own; no one else has any proprietary right in it; but if we leave out of account this royal demesne, then every acre of land is "held of" the king.[4]

Implicit in this overall concept was a kind of multiple ownership inasmuch as different persons, though, it is true, in different

---

[1] *Essays*, p. xiv.

[2] *H.E.L.*, i, 229–232.

[3] "Everywhere we see at first sight a simplicity that is truly marvellous . . . (Our Law) has been bold and strong and therefore simple" (*H.E.L.*, i, 406).

[4] *ibid.*, p. 232.

senses, might be said to hold the same land,[1] reminders of which were the lord's power of distress and the possibility that the land might escheat to him—"The tenant's interest in it might at any time expire and leave the lord's interest subsisting."[2] Of this basic concept of tenure Maitland never lost sight, and it gave a unity to his long chapter. All the same, clear and simple though the framework of the medieval land law might be, he was repeatedly at pains not to oversimplify its detail. Freedom of alienation and the creation of new tenures gave rise to all sorts of complications, and a single man might hold of different lords and by different tenures.[3] The neatly patterned feudal system and manorial system of the textbooks have no place in Maitland's account. What he did stress, however, was amongst all the complications of the later medieval land law, a curious new element of simplicity, produced by the growth of socage—"the great residuary tenure"[4]—at the expense of the other free tenures.[5]

Of all the topics treated in the *History of English Law*, tenure has secured most attention—not just from the legal, but also from the constitutional and economic, historian. This preoccupation is natural enough because of the close relationship that existed, especially in the first century after the Norman Conquest, between the feudal fief and public functions: in a brilliant phrase Disraeli once spoke of feudalism's main principle being that the tenure of property should be the fulfilment of duty, and that certainly holds good for early medieval England. So it is that the half-century since Maitland's death has seen much patient, and some distinguished, work on the problems of medieval land tenure.[6] It would be absurd to claim that this has

---

[1] *ibid.*, p. 237; see also, however, *ibid.*, ii, 4.   [2] *ibid.*, i, 355.

[3] *ibid.*, p. 296.   [4] *ibid.*, p. 294.   [5] *ibid.*, pp. 355–356.

[6] Some of the more important are—E. G. Kimball, "Judicial Aspects of Frank Almoign Tenure", *E.H.R.*, xlvii (1932); Stenton, *The First Century of English Feudalism*; H. M. Chew, *The English Ecclesiastical Tenants in Chief and Knight Service* (1932); S. Painter, *Studies in the History of the English Feudal Baronage* (1943); I. J. Sanders, *Feudal Military Service in England* (1956); J. O. Prestwich, "War and Finance in the Anglo-Norman State", *T.H.R.S.*, 5th

not added significantly to our knowledge, and equally ridiculous to attempt any sort of summary of what this addition amounts to. What can be said, however, is, first, how very much later scholars have depended on Maitland's groundwork, and, second, how rarely, in matters of real importance, they have found serious fault with it.

One tenurial topic where Maitland's interpretation has suffered modification is the very difficult matter of scutage.[1] As to its origins he wrote cautiously, though he conjectured that the supplementation of corporal service came early—from the king's point of view because the feudal host was not adequate to his needs, from the tenants' because the existence of small aliquot parts of knights' fees meant that corporal service was simply not viable. Recent work has fully justified this conjecture.[2] Where, on the other hand, his hypothesis proved less happy was about the later history of scutage, in particular about the relationship of scutage and the fine *pro servitio* which made its appearance in 1195. Theoretically, a baron who fulfilled his commitment to the crown, either by doing corporal service with the requisite number of knights or by paying scutage, was entitled to recoup himself by taking the scutage of his under-tenants; in practice, too, he obtained the writ *de scutagio habendo* to enable him to do just that. Maitland, however, thought that, after 1195, the crown's line was that the fine represented the composition of the tenant-in-chief and scutage composition of the under-tenants— in other words that scutage came to be levied as a national tax, regardless of whether service had been done or fine previously

---

series, iv (1954); E. G. Kimball, *Serjeanty Tenure in Medieval England* (1963); E. A. Kosminsky, *Studies in the Agrarian History of England in the Thirteenth Century*, trans. Kisch (1956); E. Miller, "The State and Landed Interests in Thirteenth Century France and England", *T.R.H.S.*, 5th series, ii (1952); T. F. T. Plucknett, *Legislation of Edward I* (1949); R. S. Hoyt, *The Royal Demesne in English Constitutional History*, 1066–1272 (1950).

[1] *H.E.L.*, i, 266–274.
[2] Prestwich, "War and Finance in the Anglo-Norman State", *T.R.H.S.*, 5th series, iv (1954); Hollister, "The Significance of Scutage Rates in Eleventh- and Twelfth-Century England", *E.H.R.*, lxxv (1960).

paid. So far as the first half of the thirteenth century is concerned this thesis did not survive the criticism of S. K. Mitchell, who examined the records of the reigns of John and Henry III with a thoroughness not possible for Maitland, and who came to the conclusion that fine and scutage were simply alternative methods of commutation and that scutage was not transformed into a general tax.[1] Moreover, if subsequently Miss Chew was able to show that something of the kind that Maitland envisaged did take place in Edward I's reign, thus partially rehabilitating his hypothesis, she made it clear that this change in the incidence of the levy was not, as Maitland had imagined, successfully implemented.[2]

It is probable that on no matter about which he wrote would Maitland have more readily accepted correction than on scutage. It was a subject that he approached with the greatest diffidence. On three occasions in his account of it in the *History* he stressed its difficulties, and this uncertainty is echoed in his correspondence. "I want to simplify scutage if I can," he wrote to Round on 17 December 1896, "for I don't understand it."[3] Or again, on 31 August 1898, he told Round, "At the moment I am suffering from a small relapse which is of no great consequence, but I am knowing a little of what your headaches must be and feel that scutage is a little too hard."[4]

Another matter in the history of tenure where Maitland's interpretation has been effectively challenged is the crucial statute of *Quia Emptores*. This he regarded as having been made in the interests of the king—"the one person who had all to gain and nothing to lose by the new law"[5]—and not of the magnates. Professor Plucknett has made necessary the revision of this dictum.[6] On the one hand, noting that the preamble to the statute says that it was desired by the magnates and other lords,

---

[1] S. K. Mitchell, *Taxation under John and Henry III* (1914), pp. 323–326.
[2] *E.H.R.*, xxxvii (1922), 324.
[3] *Letters*, p. 154.
[4] *ibid.*, p. 178.
[5] *H.E.L.*, i, 331 and 337 note.
[6] Plucknett, *Legislation of Edward I*, pp. 102–108.

he shows that they had indeed much to gain from it; on the other, he argues against there having been any royal plot behind *Quia Emptores* and is indeed doubtful whether the crown gained much from it.[1] On two other matters, moreover, that are connected with the statute, Professor Plucknett adds glosses of value to what Maitland wrote—first, concerning freedom of substitition, which Maitland considered a sort of *quid pro quo* for the statute's ban on subinfeudation,[2] he comments that, already before the statute was made, lords had in practice lost their power to refuse a substituted tenant; second, as to Maitland's belief that one effect of *Quia Emptores* was to prevent the creation of new manors,[3] he points out that the crown licensed subjects to create manors to be held of themselves notwithstanding the statute.

Turning from tenure to personal condition, Maitland found that, in this connection no less than in the land law, the lawyers of the thirteenth century were desirious of the greatest possible generality and simplicity. "All men are free or serfs", he states their concept. "All free men are equal; all serfs are equal:— no law of ranks can be simpler than that."[4] All the same, there were, of course, different categories of free men—earls and barons, knights, monks and clergy—that, with the special classes of aliens, Jews, outlaws and excommunicates, lepers, idiots and lunatics, women, demanded separate treatment. There were for discussion, too, the fictitious persons, the corporations that began to make for themselves a place in our law;[5] there was the

---

[1] *ibid.*, p. 105. It is possible that, in considering the long-term effects of the statute, Professor Plucknett pushes his case too far: see H. E. Bell, *An Introduction to the History and Records of the Court of Wards and Liveries* (1953), p. 50 note.

[2] *H.E.L.*, i, 337. [3] *ibid.*, p. 608. [4] *ibid.*, p. 431.

[5] A trivial, but not uninteresting, bibliographical point concerns the section of Maitland's chapter in which he dealt with fictitious persons. In the second edition of *H.E.L.* he changed the title of this section from "Fictitious Persons" to "Corporations and Churches", and added a note (at p. 486) that repeated perusal of Gierke's *Das deutsche Genossenschaftstrecht* had occasioned many changes in it. Following this note, it has been usual to cite this section, along with the section of chapter iii on Boroughs, as the main parts of *H.E.L.* in

king; and there was the vast body of the unfree that perhaps amounted to four-fifths of the total population. Nor did Maitland fail to emphasize that, despite the freeman-serf dichotomy, the line between the two became somewhat blurred. Because a fugitive serf could fairly easily obtain seisin of liberty, and because the lord's self-help in recovering him was prohibited, he had the opportunity of asserting his free status in the royal courts before judges with a confessed leaning to liberty.[1]

In comparison with the law of tenure, the medieval English law of status is poor; the modern works that have glossed Maitland's treatment of the subject are less in number, therefore, than those relating to the land law—though there is, of course, much overlap between the two.[2]

For his chapter on jurisdiction Maitland leant heavily on his own earlier work: his section on the county, for instance, included the thesis about suit of court that he had worked out in a brilliant paper as early as 1888;[3] or again, the sections on seignorial jurisdiction and the manor owed much to his introduction to the Selden volume, *Select Pleas in Manorial Courts*. The jurisdictions that he discussed were those of the land communities—shire, hundred, manor and borough—and he came up against the problem of why some of them attained personality and others did not.[4] This contrast in development, indeed,

---

which revision was undertaken for the second edition. In fact, the difference between treatment of the subject in the two editions can be exaggerated— Maitland had read, and did cite, the *Genossenschaftsrecht* in the first edition; collation between the two editions shows that the main alterations were made on the church as fictitious person, and some of these he owed to Stutz rather than Gierke.

[1] *H.E.L.*, i, 417.

[2] The following may be noted: A. L. Poole, *Obligations of Society in the 12th and 13th Centuries* (1946); N. Denholm-Young, "The Knights" in *Collected Medieval Papers*; G. C. Homans, *English Villagers of the Thirteenth Century*; L. C. Gabel, *Benefit of Clergy in the later Middle Ages* (1929); H. G. Richardson, *English Jewry under the Angevin Kings* (1960); E. H. Kantorowicz, *The King's Two Bodies* (1958).

[3] "The Suitors of the County Court", *C.P.*, i, 458–466.

[4] *H.E.L.*, i, 528.

formed the main theme of his study of jurisdiction. On the one
hand, the shire never became a corporation; though, in the reign
of Edward I, the county of Devon seems to have possessed a
common seal, the shire's unity was a matter of liabilities rather
than of rights.[1] On the other hand, the borough did achieve a
corporate personality.[2]

Since Maitland's time the land communities of medieval
England have been intensively studied by administrative and
constitutional historians.[3] In two connections there has been most
notable progress beyond the scope of his learning. First, and no
doubt the more important of the two, the franchises have been
the subject of scrupulous investigation. What Maitland termed
Edward I's "vigorous attack" on them,[4] has been set in focus by
Miss Cam, so that it now appears the climax of a century's
increasing central control.[5] Moreover, with regard to Edward's
policy, she is not disposed to accept, as Maitland was,[6] Coke's
hypothesis that the king's original idea was that every franchise,
to be valid, must be based on a royal charter, and that the statute
of *Quo Warranto* of 1290 represented a retreat from that position:
she argued that, well before the statute, franchise holders were
pleading long user as the basis of their title.[7] Second, with regard
to the lowliest of the communities, the *villata* or township,
Maitland was inclined to assign it a negative role, to do what it
was told—"The township as such has no court, no assembly."[8]
Professor W. O. Ault's studies of village by-laws, however, have

[1] *ibid.*, pp. 534–535.   [2] See above, p. 42.

[3] W. A. Morris, *The Early English County Court* (1926), *The Frankpledge
System* (1910); Cam, *The Hundred and the Hundred Rolls, Studies in the Hundred
Rolls, Liberties and Communities in Medieval England*; N. Denholm-Young,
Seignorial Administration (1937); W. O. Ault, *Private Jurisdiction in England*
(1923).

[4] *H.E.L.*, i, 572.

[5] Her work cited in note 3 above; for a valuable recent study see D. W.
Sutherland, *Quo Warranto Proceedings in the Reign of Edward I* 1279–1294(1963).

[6] *H.E.L.*, i, 572.

[7] *Liberties and Communities*, pp. 173–182; see, however, Plucknett, *Legislation of Edward I*, pp. 48–49.

[8] *H.E.L.*, i, 567.

assembled a body of evidence that suggests a good deal of activity proceeding from the farming community rather than from the lord of the manor.[1]

When he reached what he had termed the more private points of our law, the jurist became uppermost in Maitland. The approach that he made in the fourth chapter of Book II to the law of ownership and possession was characterized not only by acute understanding of its detail, but by a sympathy, almost an affection, for its subtleties. "Our interest in the land law of Henry III's day, when we regard it as private law", he said with justified pride, "will lie in this, that it is capable of becoming the land law of the England, the America, the Australia of the twentieth century."[2] That achievement was such as to call out Maitland's greatest powers, and his pages on the evolution of the doctrine of estates, his section on conveyance (especially his description of the fine),[3] and his account of the law of incorporeal things are among the most distinguished of his writings. What is so striking about them is that they seem to be written less by an historian from without than by a contemporary practitioner from within.

The crucial section of this chapter is, however, that on seisin, a topic on which Maitland had some years previously published in the *Law Quarterly Review* three of his best-known papers.[4] In those he had argued that seisin was the equivalent of possession, and this thesis he restated in the *History*. "Seisin", he said categorically, "is possession"[5] and, going on to contrast it with *jus*,

---

[1] "Some Early Village By-Laws", *E.H.R.*, xlv (1930); "Village By-Laws by Common Consent", *Speculum,* xxix (1954); see also in *International Commission for the History of Representative and Parliamentary Institutions.* xxiii, at p. 35.

[2] *H.E.L.*, ii, 1.

[3] *ibid.*, pp. 94–106. For excellent modern descriptions of the fine see R. B. Pugh, *Abstracts of Feet of Fines relating to Wiltshire for the Reigns of Edward I and Edward II*, Wilts. Arch. Soc., Records Branch, vol. I, introduction; *Calendar of Kent Feet of Fines to the end of Henry III's Reign*, Kent. Arch. Soc., Records Branch, vol. xv, introduction by Frank W. Jessup.

[4] "The Seisin of Chattels", "The Mystery of Seisin", "The Beatitude of Seisin". They are reprinted in *C.P.*, i.

[5] *H.E.L.*, ii, 29.

M.–F

it is "sharply opposed to proprietary right".[1] Some thirty years later Joüon des Longrais queried the validity of the definition and denied that the dichotomy that Maitland thought he saw had really existed.[2] Seisin was not *possessio*, nor *jus proprietas*. Instead, "*Jus* et *saisina* sont également taillés dans une même étoffe, c'est le droit réel antérieur s'exprimant surtout par la jouissance, la seule conception que le moyen âge entende pleinement."[3] In other words, the two are relative, and closely interconnected, terms: every right is a sort of potential seisin, and seisin a right that has materialized. Where Maitland seems to have gone wrong, apart from following the teaching of Heusler,[4] is, more significantly, in an undue dependence on Bracton. For two reasons Bracton was an unsafe guide—first because his Romanism led him to speak of possession and ownership in a way that did not really chime with contemporary English law; second because, by the time he wrote, the existence for three-quarters of a century of the "possessory" assizes had produced a superficial contrast between seisin and proprietary right that was based on procedure and not on substantive law.

Some have gone farther than this and regretted that Maitland took over from Bracton the term possessory assizes. It has been argued that it was not Henry II's intention to create separate sets of remedies for two distinct kinds of title, possession and ownership; he did not merely make possession nine points of the law, for he took care that his new remedies should not protect wrongful seisins—that is, those seisins that were protected had in them some element of right.[5] In any event, however it may be with regard to Henry II, the long-term trend of our law is clear: certainly by the end of the thirteenth century no dichotomy between seisin and right existed, for the action of right was

---

[1] *ibid.*, p. 33.

[2] F. Joüon des Longrais, *La Conception anglaise de la Saisine* (1925).

[3] *ibid.*, p. 57.

[4] A. Heusler, *Gewere*.

[5] R. C. Van Caenegem, *Royal Writs in England from the Conquest to Glanvill*, Selden Soc., vol. 77, especially pp. 306–313; Naomi D. Hurnard, "Did Edward I reverse Henry II's Policy upon Seisin?" *E.H.R.*, lxix (1954); Plucknett, *Legislation of Edward I*, pp. 53–55, *contra*.

practically out of use and virtually it was the oldest seisin that constituted the best right. In a way Maitland's treatment of the subject, based as it was on his definition of seisin as possession, masked the essential unity of the medieval land law—though it is fair to add that he was by no means unaware of those aspects of the problem that more recent writers have stressed.[1]

About the *History*'s chapter on contract it is not necessary to say much, for contract was long in attaining its dominance in English law, and the authors were concerned, therefore, only with the origins—almost, it might be said, with the prehistory—of this branch of our law. As Maitland put it after citing Bracton's treatment of the subject, "the main lesson that we learn from it is that at the end of Henry III's reign our king's court has no general doctrine of contract".[2] The most interesting parts of this chapter are perhaps those that deal with the clash of jurisdiction between the ecclesiastical and temporal courts—with the fifteenth chapter of the Constitutions of Clarendon, the writs of prohibition, and the so-called statute *Circumspecte agatis*[3]—and with the evolution of the seal.[4]

His discussion of inheritance Maitland opened with a lucid twenty pages—"filled rather by warnings than by theories"[5]— on the antiquities of the subject. They are marked by a cool, and eminently common-sense, criticism of the facile generalization of the anthropological school that the family rather than the individual was the unit of ancient law. In the earliest rules about inheritance and the blood feud, the dead man's kinsfolk, who are to bear the feud and share the wergild, are partly paternal, partly maternal, relations, and the significance of this is obvious—

[1] e.g. "To our medieval lawyers the word *seisina* suggested the very opposite of violence; it suggested peace and quiet" (*H.E.L.*, ii, 30). ". . . . it seems constantly assumed in our books that the possessory remedy exists chiefly for the benefit of those who have good title" (*ibid.*, p. 46). "Every title to land has its root in seisin; the title which has its root in the oldest seisin is the best title" (*ibid.*).

[2] *H.E.L.*, ii, 194.

[3] *ibid.*, pp. 198–202; for a good modern account of *Circumspecte agatis* see E. B. Graves, "Circumspecte Agatis", *E.H.R.*, xliii (1928).

[4] *H.E.L.*, ii, 223–224.   [5] *ibid.*, p. 240.

"when we see that the wives of the members of one clan are themselves members of other clans, we ought not to talk of clans at all".[1] Here is a system scarcely compatible with rigid and mutually exclusive kin groups. The same conclusion Maitland reached from his discussion of family ownership, which he showed to have been, in all probability, less something original than the outcome of intestate succession: the extent to which the interest of the expectant heir was protected fluctuated, but it did not steadily decrease.

Coming to the post-Conquest period, where he felt able to move with greater certainty, Maitland listed and discussed six rules of inheritance which by the end of Henry III's reign applied. The most central and significant of them was the rule of primogeniture. This, he pointed out, was no part of the natural law of inheritance. Rather—amongst the holders of military fiefs, where it originated—it was due to the necessity, for reasons of convenience, of impartible descent. Yet if the descent of the fief as an integral whole had advantages for the lord, it had its dangers, too, and absolute primogeniture, as it appeared in England, was only possible because there existed so highly centralized a feudalism that the king did not fear unduly the power of even his mightiest vassals. So it was that Maitland dated the acceptance of primogeniture, not from the Norman Conquest, as had been generally held, nor even from the period of Anglo-Norman rule, but from the strong, confident reign of Henry II:

> The last years of Henry II were the years that decided the matter for good and all, and they were years in which a newly fashioned court, unhampered by precedents, was with rude, youthful vigour laying down its first principles. Here as elsewhere its work is characterized by a bold, an almost reckless, simplicity. Nor must we fail to note that here as elsewhere it generalized the law of the great folk and made it common law for all free and lawful men, except some ancient and dwindling classes which had hardly come within its ken.[2]

This dating has been subject to some criticism. On the one

[1] *ibid.*, p. 242.   [2] *ibid.*, p. 274.

hand, Professor Génestal has argued that in the eleventh century the Normans knew primogeniture and that it was with them the dominant, if not exclusive, system.[1] On the other hand, Professor S. E. Thorne, in the first of the Maitland Memorial Lectures that he delivered in Cambridge in 1959,[2] has contended that what led Maitland to place the acceptance of primogeniture as late as Henry II's time was his desire to account for the disappearance, directly after that date, of the need to obtain consent of the expectant heirs before land was conveyed away. That rule, according to Maitland, had owed its existence to the partibility of the inheritance: its intention had been to secure equal division amongst sons. But it was no longer necessary, was indeed patently unjust, when the new law of primogeniture gave the eldest son, at his father's death, the whole of his father's land. So it was that free alienation without the heir's consent followed as a consequence of primogeniture.[3] That thesis Professor Thorne is disposed to reject, putting in its place the theory that until the very end of the twelfth century the military fief was not heritable, being merely an estate for life: if the gift was to continue after the tenant's death, the consent of his heir to any alienation was naturally necessary: on the other hand, with heritability, and the full ownership that it implied, consent to alienation was no longer required. For Professor Thorne, therefore, free alienation follows from heritability, not from primogeniture, and he is thus able to argue against the postponement of primogeniture to Maitland's late date for it.[4]

---

[1] R. Génestal, "La Formation du droit d'ainesse", *Normannia*, i.

[2] *Cambridge Law Journal*, 1959.

[3] *H.E.L.*, ii, 308–309.

[4] Professor Thorne regards as the "basic flaw" in Maitland's analysis his assumption that military fiefs were heritable from the Conquest or soon thereafter. Yet his own postponement of heritability to 1200 is, in some ways, hard to accept. Mr Brian Simpson's comment has point—that Professor Thorne's problem is definitional: "How scanty have the lord's rights over the land to become before one can say that the tenant's heir inherits?" (A. W. B. Simpson, *An Introduction to the History of the Land Law* (1961), p. 47 note). Of this difficulty Maitland was well aware—"There is hardly a strict right to inherit when there is no settled rule about reliefs, and the heir must make the

The most notable feature of Maitland's treatment of family law is the graceful essay that it includes on marriage, the principal importance of which was that it led him on to those inquiries that bore fruit in his *Roman Canon Law in the Church of England*.[1] Although the royal courts had much to say about dower and inheritance—both of them matters that were closely connected with marriage—they were not concerned with marriage as such, which was the business of the church. Nor did she conduct that business very satisfactorily. Maitland, indeed, showed the church treating marriage as a formless contract and at the same time multiplying impediments so recklessly as to make the formation of a valid marriage into something almost accidental.[2] About the affinities that the church devised he was particularly critical. "Behind these intricate rules", he put it, "there is no deep policy, there is no strong religious feeling; they are the idle ingenuities of men who are amusing themselves by inventing a game of skill which is to be played with neatly drawn tables of affinity and doggerel hexameters."[3] Nor did he approve of the way in which the church courts handled matrimonial causes that came before them. Having described a particularly un-savoury case that reached the royal court on petitition for dower in 1302, he confessed that it left him feeling it hard to believe that the ecclesiastical courts were pre-eminently fit to administer the law of marriage and divorce.[4] "He disliked ecclesiasticism," Maitland's friend, Buckland, said of him, "and, on the whole, for him the presumption was against a clergyman."[5] But in this particular context the presumption was justified.

---

best bargain that he can with the king" (*H.E.L.*, ii, 266). The circumstances of the post-Conquest period did not make for precise conditions of tenure (see the examples, for then and later, in Reginald Lennard, *Rural England* 1086–1135, p. 112). "The truth is that men gave lands and took lands and left the terms of the tenure to be decided thereafter by the course of events and their own strong wills" (*H.E.L.*, i, 316).

[1] See below, ch. VIII.   [2] *H.E.L.*, ii, 385.   [3] *ibid.*, p. 389.
[4] *ibid.*, p. 396.
[5] W. W. Buckland, "F. W. Maitland", *Cambridge Law Journal*, i, 293.

The aim of Maitland's chapter on crime and tort was comparatively modest, for it was not his plan to traverse ground that was already adequately covered, and the criminal law had been fortunate in its historians. For the law as it had developed by the later Middle Ages there were two good books—one ancient, Hale's *Pleas of the Crown*, and one recent, Sir James Fitzjames Stephen's *History of the Criminal Law*—and for Teutonic origins there was Brunner's *Deutsche Rechtsgeschichte*. "There are admirable books at our right hand and at our left", Maitland confessed. "Our endeavour will be to build a bridge between them."[1]

He opened his chapter, therefore, with a quite short and slight sketch of the ancient criminal law. This was attractively written and comparable, in the neatness of its organization, to his sections on the antiquities of inheritance and on marriage in earlier chapters of the *History*. It was, however, less successful than either of these. It was marred by Maitland's exaggeration of the extent to which the crown, in late Old English times, had alienated its jurisdictional rights.[2] Again, although Maitland saw that there were connections between the *bots* and the ecclesiastical system of penance, he did not stop to work these out in any detail.[3] Finally, whilst he stressed the adverse effects of *bot* and *wite*,[4] he failed to see that they at least meant that the Saxon criminal law included an effective provision for reparation that was lacking in our later law—a point recently well put by Professor Plucknett: "We must lament that in the twelfth century we acquired that dangerous gift of a little learning, and so we discovered how to draw a firm line between crime and tort; as a result we awarded reparation in tort but not in crime."[5]

For the rest, the chapter consisted of three sections—felony and treason, the trespasses, and ecclesiastical offences. Of these the first and third may be briefly dealt with. Maitland found it

---

[1] *H.E.L.*, ii, 448.

[2] *ibid.*, pp. 453–455; see above, p. 29.

[3] *H.E.L.*, ii, 452 and 476; see T. P. Oakley, *English Penitential Discipline and Anglo-Saxon Law in their Joint Influence* (1923).

[4] *H.E.L.*, ii, 460.

[5] Plucknett, *Edward I and Criminal Law*, p. 23.

necessary to define felony by its legal effects rather than in absolute terms, and indeed, when treason slowly came to be distinguished from felony, it, too, was marked off by different legal consequences from those that followed felony. The most notable feature of this section was its discussion of culpability in medieval law and of the slowness with which the criminal law came to concern itself with intention in crime. As to ecclesiastical offences, the problems relative to the chief of them, heresy, Maitland saw were academic, for within the period with which he was concerned England was too little troubled by heresy for any settled course of procedure to emerge. In any event, more important than the detail of this chapter is the warning with which Maitland concluded it, that crimes of violence were common and that the criminal law was exceedingly inefficient. The predominance of outlawry over punishment was the confession of the law's failure.[1]

Trespass it is necessary to discuss rather more fully, for Maitland's views as to the origin of that "fertile mother of actions"[2] have been substantially modified by recent scholarship. Despite a saver that some early precedents might be found for it, he thought that the action emerged during Henry III's last years[3] and, as to ancestry, that it was closely connected with the appeal for felony—"The action of trespass", he claimed, "is, we may say, an attenuated appeal", because, in its early days, it was aimed at genuine breaches of the king's peace.[4] There are here, then, two points—one as to date, the other as to derivation. As to the first, Mr Richardson and Professor Sayles have shown that the actual writ of trespass appears to have been introduced about the beginning of Henry III's reign,[5] but that, before then, actions of trespass, begun by plaint, were by no means infre-

---

[1] H.E.L., ii, 557; see also, ibid., p. 583.   [2] ibid., p. 525.

[3] ibid. In The Forms of Action he says "about 1250", but admits that instances of such actions are found in John's reign (Equity also the Forms of Action at Common Law, pp. 342–343).

[4] H.E.L., ii, 526.

[5] Select Cases of Procedure without Writ under Henry III, Selden Soc., vol. 60, p. cxv.

quent on the plea rolls.[1] They believe that the ultimate origin of trespass lies far back in the history of English law.[2] With regard to the second point, the action's derivation, there, too, Maitland's theory that trespass stemmed from the appeal, although advanced independently by Holmes and Ames, has been challenged. Woodbine has sought to connect it with *novel disseisin*;[3] Richardson and Sayles attribute to it a very ancient origin alongside the appeal of felony,[4] but with the Roman law *actio iniuriarum* an important influence on its evolution.[5] Most fundamental of all is Mr Milsom's thesis.[6] He queries the validity of Maitland's view that trespass was a concept involving direct force, and argues convincingly that the *vi et armis*, alleged in the writ, was from the first a formality and not the vestigial trace of an earlier, genuine complaint.[7] Trespass, he holds, never meant anything narrower than wrong,[8] and what was significant about its appearance in the royal courts was not that they were inventing a new remedy so much as that they were getting their hand on to a type of grievance previously remedied in the local courts.[9] This interpretation overturns Maitland's theory. It is worth noting, however, that (as so frequently happens in connection with Maitland's work) a hint of the better opinion that has now replaced his can be found in his own account. Describing the slowness and difficulty with which the royal court gave an action against the smith or surgeon whose inefficiency had tortious consequences, he went on, "We may well doubt whether Bracton or any contemporary lawyer would have told them that they had committed no tort, we may perhaps doubt whether they could not have been successfully sued in some of the local courts; but the king's justices were not as yet busied with these questions. . . ."[10]

---

[1] *ibid.*, p. cviii.   [2] *ibid.*, p. cxxxii.

[3] Woodbine, "Origins of the Action of Trespass", *Yale Law Journal*, xxxiii and xxxiv.

[4] *op. cit.*, p. cxxxii.   [5] *ibid.*, p. cxvi.

[6] S. F. C. Milsom, "Trespass from Henry III to Edward III", *L.Q.R.*, lxxiv (1958).

[7] *ibid.*, p. 196.   [8] *ibid.*, p. 583.   [9] *ibid.*   [10] *H.E.L.*, ii, 527.

In the final chapter of the *History*, on procedure, the two most important sections are those dealing with the forms of action and with pleading and proof.

The forms of action were, of course, of crucial significance in the development of the medieval common law. From the king's point of view the original writs were the means whereby justice became centralized and the royal courts drew business away from other courts; from the subjects' point of view they were the means by which the new commissioned royal justice and the benefit of the sworn inquest were placed at the disposal of anyone who could bring his case within a certain formula—that is, who could obtain an appropriate writ to start his action. In the period of just over a hundred years between the accession of Henry II and the death of Henry III, with which in the *History* Maitland was principally concerned, the numbers of stereotyped writs (*de cursu*) that were available, and therefore the scope of royal justice, greatly increased: by the reign of Edward I there were some five hundred writs on the Register. This was the time when, as Maitland put it, the Chancery was "doling out actions one by one",[1] and when it was possible for Bracton to say that "Tot erunt formulae brevium quot sunt genera actionum".[2] Towards the end of the century, as it came to be realized that the power to create new remedies was in effect the power to make law, a brake was put on the creation of new original writs and the formulary system hardened. But Glanville, by building his book round the writs, had been influential in making them central to English law.

"Knowledge of the procedure in the various forms of action", Maitland said, "is the core of English medieval jurisprudence."[3] It was a topic which concerned him much. As early as 1890 he had contributed a paper on the history of the Register to the *Harvard Law Review*[4] and the formulary system was the subject of the best of all his lecture courses, posthumously published as *The Forms of Action at Common Law*.[5] In view of this, his treat-

---

[1] *ibid.*, ii, 559.   [2] Cited *ibid.*, ii, 560 note.
[3] *Equity also the Forms of Action at Common Law*, p. 303.
[4] *C.P.*, ii, 110–173.   [5] See below, App.

ment of the forms of action in the *History of English Law* was disappointing: it was short and not comprehensive. That this was so was due to a number of factors. First, the plan of the *History* had left procedure to the very end, and, when he reached it, it is possible that his energies were beginning to flag. Again, and most notably, this subject more than any other suffered from the division of the *History* into its two Books, chronological and analytical, which involved him, so far as the formulary system was concerned, in taking two bites at one cherry. Finally, there is about what he wrote in the *History* the hint of a desire not to repeat what he had already said. Perhaps, too, the fact is that, with a terminal date of 1272, the forms of action could not be adequately treated: the history of the lawyers' rather fruitless attempt to classify them, for instance, took him beyond the range of the *History*, and he dealt with it more successfully elsewhere.[1] However it may be as to the reasons for it, Maitland's teaching on the forms of action is better sought in the lectures and the Harvard paper than in the *History of English Law*.

At two points that teaching has suffered modification at the hands of later scholarship, both of them relating, curiously enough, to the most frequently cited contemporary maxims about the medieval writ system. The first is the famous rule, *Nemo tenetur respondere sine brevi*. This Maitland attributed to "some ordinance lost to us" of Henry II, designed merely to protect seisin, and not touching the question of proprietary right.[2] The hypothesis has not met with acceptance; it has been pointed out that there is no evidence for the existence of any such ordinance, that Glanvill expressly states the rule to have been customary, and that it represented an entirely natural psychological development.[3] The other maxim is Bracton's complement to this first rule, *Non potest quis sine brevi agere*. In a

[1] *The Forms of Action at Common Law*, ch. VII; "Historical Note on the Classification of the Forms of Personal Action", *Pollocks's Law of Torts*, 14th edn., App. A.

[2] *Equity also the Forms of Action at Common Law*, pp. 25–28.

[3] Van Caenegem, *Royal Writs in England from the Conquest to Glanvill*, Selden Soc., vol. 77, pp. 223–224.

sense this was the springboard for Maitland's interpretation; but it is a text on which, since his time, Mr Richardson and Professor Sayles have presented an illuminating commentary in their *Select Cases of Procedure without Writ under Henry III*.[1] They show that the *querela*, or plaint, was another means of seeking remedy than the writs issued by chancery; the plaint antedated procedure by writ, and, especially with the increasing rigidity of the formulary system, was an important way of supplementing procedure by writ.[2]

If the account of the forms of action in the *History of English Law* is not wholly satisfactory, that cannot be said of the section on pleading and proof, which, nearly three-quarters of a century after it was written, remains the *locus classicus* for the history of ancient methods of proof and the emergence of the jury. Starting with the odd paradox—to modern eyes—that under the ancient system judgment preceded proof, Maitland showed how a nascent rationalism began to make itself felt in the decision as to which of the two parties to a suit must go to the proof and to what proof he must go.[3] In the reign of Henry II a new mode of proof appeared, that of the sworn inquest of neighbours. Originally the recognitors in the petty assizes were summoned to give a simple answer to a straightforward question; but should a defendant, without making a full denial of the plaintiff's allegation, wish to raise an *exceptio* to it, they might well be required to answer another question as to the validity of the facts alleged in the *exceptio*.[4] "The extension of the *exceptio*", Maitland says, "is the extension of a new mode of proof; it is the extension of a mode of proof which will become famous under the name of trial by jury."[5] What is important—and indeed this is perhaps the most significant part of Maitland's thesis—is the form that the inquest took in England, emerging in quite emphatic contrast to the inquisitory procedure of the church.[6]

To this account of the *History of English Law* there may be added a few words by way of generalization about the characteristics of the book.

---

[1] Selden Soc., vol. 60. [2] *ibid.*, p. xiv. [3] *H.E.L.*, ii, 603.
[4] *ibid.*, p. 617. [5] *ibid.*, p. 616. [6] *ibid.*, pp. 656–659.

As to its content one point may be underlined. Any full-scale history of medieval law must, of course, include widely diverse material; yet Maitland's recognition of a number of central and recurrent themes in that history gave an overall unity to his book. One such theme was what he termed the "beautiful simplicity"[1] of the law of the twelfth and thirteenth centuries— a basic simplicity that he found alike in the law of tenure, personal status and inheritance. He was insistent that his reader should not project the overelaboration of the late medieval centuries back into Angevin times:

> Now subtlety is the very last quality for which we should either blame or praise the justices who under Henry II and his sons built up the first courses of our common law. Those who charge them, and even their predecessors of the Norman reigns, with subtlety are too often confusing the work of the fifteenth century with the work of the twelfth, and ascribing it all to "Norman Lawyers":— they might as well ascribe flamboyant tracery to architects of the Norman age.[2]

Another recurrent theme—or perhaps Maitland would have regarded it as simply an aspect of the first—was the tendency of the law for the great men to become, too, the law for the small. That was the significance of the king's court as it emerged from the period of Henry II's reforms;[3] that was what made it interesting that, by the end of the thirteenth century, the free man usually had a seal;[4] that was why the generalization of primogeniture to all freeholders really mattered.[5] Again, Maitland saw as one of the central questions of English history the relationship of the common law with Roman law, and in his introductory chapter claimed that he had tried to keep before his reader the problem of why Roman law did not maintain its influence in this country.[6] The claim was justified: not only did he give Roman law its own chapter in the first Book, but in famous passages he considered its influence on Glanvill[7] and on Bracton,[8] and his index contains some seventy references to it.

---

[1] ibid., p. 274.   [2] ibid., p. 446.   [3] ibid., i, 153.   [4] ibid., ii, 224.
[5] ibid., p. 274.   [6] ibid., i, p. xxxiv.   [7] ibid., pp. 165–166.
[8] ibid., pp. 223–225.

For the rest, the most notable features of the *History of English Law* are the wide range and intensive learning of the book and the graceful elegance with which Maitland deployed that learning. In our own age we are familiar with a high standard of record scholarship and an impressive command of archival detail over a narrow field; in all ages the *savant*, with a wide knowledge of the publications of foreign scholars, is a sufficiently familiar figure. What is, and always must be, rare is the combination in a single man of both sorts of scholarship, especially in the degree to which Maitland possessed them. To the material he had himself quarried from medieval records he somehow found time to add a precise knowledge of the work of continental scholars like Esmein and Savigny, Brunner and Gierke. Yet for all the European scholarship that gave depth and background to his work, in its presentation Maitland contrived to be "mere English". What would a German scholar make of his description of the functions of the judge within the context of medieval English formalism?

> We are often reminded of the cricket-match. The judges sit in court, not in order that they may discover the truth, but in order that they may answer the question, "How's that?"[1]

Finally, parts of the *History of English Law* are, simply judged by literary standards, outstandingly fine writing. It would be wrong to add to a chapter, already perhaps over-heavily laced with direct quotation, further extracts to prove the point. But the opening paragraph of Maitland's chapter on the Norman kings;[2] the sentences in which he described the forms of action as living things;[3] above all, the noble concluding pages of the *History*[4]—these, and so much else, are worthy of a place in any anthology of English prose.

---

[1] *ibid.*, ii, 671. One thinks, too, of his description of the acre in *Domesday Book and Beyond*, p. 372—"The breadth of the acre is still known to all Englishmen, for it is the distance between the wickets."

[2] *H.E.L.*, i, 79.

[3] *ibid.*, ii, 561.

[4] *ibid.*, pp. 672–674.

VI

THE ORIGINS OF PARLIAMENT

THE origins of parliament, especially that facet of them with which Maitland was most concerned, are closely connected with one of the topics discussed in the last chapter—the king's duty to right wrongs and the development of the means by which he did so. The notion of the *complementum iustitiae*, the reserve of justice that remained in the crown over and beyond the operation of the royal courts, has an important relationship to our parliamentary origins.

What came to be the normal procedure for a free man who was, or felt himself to be, wronged was to obtain an appropriate writ and seek justice in one or other of the king's courts. Through the thirteenth century there was a great increase of writs *de cursu*, or, putting it rather differently, of formulae within which the litigant, desirous of the benefits of royal justice, might bring his case.[1] Yet even that increase, notable though it was, was not enough: inevitably there remained a wide field where no suitable writ was available, and this was felt to be no reason why justice should go by default. Hence the pleas without writ—by plaint, *querela* and *querimonia*—which, older than the writ system itself, enjoyed in the late thirteenth and fourteenth centuries a widely extended use,[2] and hence, too, and most important of all, procedure by petition. Petitions were often concerned with matters where the king's own interests were involved, and they were sometimes seeking redress as of grace and not as of right. Amongst the public records Maitland found some 15,000 of

[1] See above, p. 82.
[2] Richardson and Sayles, *Select Cases of Procedure without Writ under Henry III*, Selden Soc., vol. 60, p. xiv.

them, dating from the thirteenth to the fifteenth century, in the class called ancient petitions, and a further 1,000 in the class known as ancient petitions, exchequer:[1] a more recent estimate puts the total at upwards of 20,000.[2] A great proportion of them, though not all, were dealt with in parliament.

On 6 January 1889 Maitland accepted the invitation of Maxwell-Lyte, the Deputy Keeper of the Records, to edit a volume of petitions to parliament in the Rolls Series. The way in which that proposed volume changed into an edition of the parliament roll of 1305 is described by Miss Cam in the introduc-tion to her edition of the *Selected Historical Essays of F. W. Maitland*,[3] nor does a re-examination of the correspondence between Maitland and Maxwell-Lyte add very much to what she says. The determining fact was that the dating of the petitions presented marked difficulties. For such of them as possessed a dated endorsement the question did not arise; dating was pos-sible, too, where the petition was enclosed with a dated writ or could be associated with a dated enrolment. But the first category formed a small minority, and for particular reasons there were not as many in the second and third categories as might have been expected. As to enclosure within a dated document, it was un-fortunate that, at the time of the creation of the class of ancient petitions, many had been separated from the warrants and inquisitions to which they belonged; and as to association with a dated enrolment, it must be remembered that in Maitland's time, little had so far been done to calendar the chancery rolls. To add to these difficulties, when, under Sir Francis Palgrave, the peti-tions had been rearranged, old wrappers and labels had been destroyed. So it was that Maitland found himself on the horns of a dilemma. "I should not like to have before me", he wrote on 27 June 1889, "the alternative of publishing nothing for six years or of being hurried into publishing some slovenly work."[4]

[1] *M. de P.*, xxvi.
[2] G. L. Haskins, "The Petitions of Representatives in the Parliaments of Edward I", *E.H.R.*, liii (1938), 5.
[3] pp. xv–xvi.
[4] Maitland to Maxwell-Lyte, *Letters*, p. 68.

Nor apparently did he escape from this alternative by the plan he mooted the following August. That was to print first such petitions as could be firmly assigned to particular years of Edward I's reign, and then those which appeared from internal evidence to belong to some part of the reign. When even this modified approach appeared unsatisfactory, on 1 October he put up a proposal, which the Deputy Keeper accepted, that an edition of the parliament roll of 1305 should replace that of the petitions. "It seems to me", he wrote in a long, carefully reasoned letter, "that one Parliament Roll, edited with the original petitions and the consequent writs, would be an excellent forerunner for a calendar of petitions."[1] Transcription of the roll, parts of which, as a matter of fact, were already in print, presented no particular difficulty and, with W. P. Baildon's aid, this part of the work was near completion by November.

Even this last scheme of Maitland's, however, ran up against the difficulty of locating the relevant petitions. Two whole years later he was asking how the cataloguing of petitions was proceeding—"I made some inquiries in September but understood that I had better wait."[2] In view of the frustrations of the work, his comments on the activities of his predecessors, as they appeared in his introduction, are extraordinarily mild.[3] "I have said as little as I could," he wrote to Maxwell-Lyte on 14 January 1893, "but, do what I can, I can not altogether avoid the suggestion that bundles were broken up without enough care being taken to preserve evidence of their contents. . . . Such is my admiration for Palgrave that I do not like saying anything that anybody, however perverse, could twist into blame. I have written some pages over and over again without satisfying myself."[4] Maitland was a remarkably generous man.

It is fair to add that, as well as the hold-up over the petitions, there were other factors that made for delay in the completion of his edition. One of them was worsening health. In the autumn of 1891 he found it necessary to warn Maxwell-Lyte that he had to work under so many restrictions imposed by doctors that he

[1] *ibid.*, p. 71. [2] 29 Nov. 1891, *Letters*, p. 97.
[3] *M. de P.*, pp. xxviii–xxix. [4] *Letters*, p. 111.

M.–G

found it impossible to promise what he would do in the future,[1] and some four months later he wrote to Fisher—"I ought to be at the Record Office among the parliamentary petitions—but can only do a day's work now and then."[2] Beyond even this, the guess may be hazarded that the task in which he had become involved interested him less than his Selden Society commitments. He confessed to Vinogradoff as early as August 1889— barely six months after his appointment as editor—that his hope was to start the edition of petitions and then get out of it.[3] Whatever relative weight should be assigned to these various causes of delay, the *Memoranda de Parliamento* did not, in fact, appear until 1893—for Maitland, who worked fast, an abnormally long time.

In choosing to define his task as he did, Maitland was, in one sense, not breaking new ground, for from the early fourteenth century onwards record-keepers and others had worked on the parliament rolls, originally for official, and later for academic, purposes. The list begins as early as 1322 with the *liber de parliamentis*, thought to be identical with the *Vetus Codex*, so much used by later editors of the parliament rolls: the *Vetus Codex* contains an apparently random selection of the rolls of the parliaments of Edward I and Edward II.[4] Towards the end of the sixteenth century an abstract of the parliament rolls in his custody was made by William Bowyer, the keeper of the records in the Tower of London, while his successor, Michael Heneage, may have made an actual transcript of them. In 1657 Bowyer's abstract was published, and in 1661 William Ryley's *Placita Parliamentaria*. Ultimately, in implementation of a house of lords resolution of 1767, the six volumes of *Rotuli Parliamentorum* appeared in 1783, and a further five rolls were printed by Henry Cole in the Record Commission's *Documents Illustrative of English History in the Thirteenth and Fourteenth Centuries*.[5]

[1] 29 Nov. 1891, *ibid.*, p. 97.

[2] 24 Mar. 1892, *ibid.*, p. 69.

[3] 27 Aug. 1889, *ibid.*, p. 69.

[4] Richardson and Sayles, "The Early Records of the English Parliaments", *B.I.H.R.*, vi (1928–9), 137.

[5] Richardson and Sayles, *Rotuli parliamentorum Anglie hactenus inediti, 1279–1373*, Camden Soc., 3rd series, li (1935), pp. xxii–xxvii.

It was, indeed, with some mixed feelings that Maitland came to his decision to republish the roll of 1305, for he recognized that there was much to be said against reprinting what was already in print and accessible to scholars. Two sets of factors, however, reconciled him to doing so. On the one hand, he became aware of the inadequacy of the existing edition. "One discovers gradually", he told Round, "that the editors of the Parliament Roll never used an original document when they could find a late transcript of it",[1] and, so far as his own roll was concerned, he knew from their own words that they had used third-hand materials.[2] On the other hand, as we have already noticed in his letter to Maxwell-Lyte, he became attracted by the possibility of bringing together roll, original petitions, and resultant writs—a theme he developed in his introduction.[3]

The text of Maitland's *Memoranda de Parliamento* has the technical excellence of his other, both earlier and later, editorial work. Mr Richardson and Professor Sayles have made detailed criticism of his views regarding the intermixture of Lent and Michaelmas petitions on the roll,[4] nor do they believe that all the petitions he edited belonged to one parliament as he imagined.[5] Again, quite recently two additional membranes, of like character to the rest of the roll, have been added to it.[6] These, however, are not large matters. What was typical of Maitland's editing, the provision of ancillary material, designed to make interpretation of the text more easy, is a notable feature of the *Memoranda*. It contains a calendar of the parliament, lists of the household, council, courts, ministers, principal lawyers, sheriffs and assembly of estates, as well as a classified list of petitions, an index of persons and an index of places. Above all, it includes his very interesting introduction, with its stress on the audience of petitions amongst his parliament's functions and on the king's council amongst the elements participating in it.

It has become customary to regard Maitland's introduction to

[1] 10 April 1892, *Letters*, p. 100.
[2] *M. de P.*, p. xii.   [3] *ibid.*, p. xxvii.
[4] *B.I.H.R.*, vi, 149.   [5] *L.Q.R.*, lxxvii (1961), 413.
[6] *ibid.*, note.

the *Memoranda* as not merely a milestone, but also as a turning-point in the study of parliamentary origins.[1] In this connection, however, Maitland's position in parliamentary historiography has perhaps been misunderstood. There are several reasons for thinking that the formative character of his introduction has been overemphasized.

The first of them is that Maitland did not, of course, "discover" either the judicial function of early parliaments or the crucial importance of the conciliar element in them. Both characteristics had been stressed as early as 1819 in the *Reports from the Lords' Committees . . . touching the Dignity of a Peer*. More significantly their central importance in parliamentary origins had been clearly brought out by L. O. Pike in his editions of the Year Books of 12 and 13, and 13 and 14, Edward III. In the former he had drawn attention to a remarkable instance of petitions to the king in his council in his parliament;[2] in the latter, discussing the case of Staunton *v.* Staunton and wife, he had commented—"The moment any insufficiency appears, justice has to be aided from the source from which it originally flows, the king in his Council in his Parliament, through the appropriate channel, the Chancery."[3] Even Stubbs, however little he let it affect his central argument, was aware of the mass of work involved in dealing with petitions, and that this work was done by the council in parliament.[4] In view of these distinguished predecessors it is difficult to describe what Maitland did as "trail-blazing".[5]

Again, the sort of claim that has been made for Maitland in this connection would, in his view, have conflicted with what he took to be his duty as an editor. "Even if he had settled opinions about debatable questions of constitutional history," he wrote specifically in the introduction under discussion, "it would be wrong for the editor of such a book as this is to thrust them

[1] See, for example, Erskine May, *Parliamentary Practice* (14th ed. by Sir G. Campion, 1946), p. 1.

[2] *Year Books of the Reign of King Edward III, Years XII and XIII*, p. xciv seq.

[3] *Year Books of the Reign of King Edward III, Years XIII and XIV*, pp. xliii–xliv.

[4] *Constitutional History of England*, 4th edn., ii, 275–277.

[5] *A.H.R.*, lvii (1951–2), 318.

forward. The most that he can legitimately do is to provide materials for the formation of opinions."[1] Add to this his own almost pathological modesty and the probability, argued above, that his parliamentary studies took a comparatively low priority amongst his current interests, and the tentativeness of his introduction is understandable. It is interesting; it is suggestive. But it is not definitive. As Mr Miller has remarked very sensibly, "He was introducing a set of documents and not rewriting the history of parliament."[2]

Moreover, though the hypotheses he advanced have, of course, had a significant influence on the subsequent study of parliamentary origins, it is important to understand aright the nature of that influence and, above all, not to exaggerate its directness. Certainly it was not immediate. On publication the *Memoranda* caused no stir, and in the next fifteen years such impact as it had was less on parliamentary than on council history. It is true that, in 1910, with C. H. McIlwain's *High Court of Parliament*, which its author tells us grew out of a paper on Maitland,[3] there began a quarter of a century's stress on the judicial functions of early parliaments. It was the judicial element in them that A. F. Pollard stressed, with particular recognition of Maitland's work as his starting-point,[4] in his *Evolution of Parliament*—an inaccurate, but popular, book which Gaillard Lapsley used to refer to as "Mr Pollard's sprightly pamphlet". More important, in the same decade there began to appear a long series of contributions to parliamentary history by Mr H. G. Richardson and Professor G. O. Sayles, which were much concerned with the judicial strand in parliament's development.[5] That was the preoccupation, too, of an important paper by Mr J. E. A. Jolliffe.[6] All this was, in

[1] *M. de P.*, p. lxxxiv.

[2] E. Miller, *The Origins of Parliament* (Hist. Assoc., 1960), p. 6.

[3] *High Court of Parliament* (1910), p. xiii.

[4] *Evolution of Parliament* (1920, 2nd ed. 1926), p. v.

[5] Richardson and Sayles, "Parliaments and Great Councils in Medieval England", *L.Q.R.*, lxxvii (1961), 224 note, for list of their principal contributions.

[6] J. E. A. Jolliffe, "Some Factors in the Beginning of Parliament", *T.R.H.S.*, 4th series, xxii (1940).

a sense, derivative from ideas discussed in Maitland's introduction to the *Memoranda*. Nevertheless it must be kept in mind that his successors—and especially Mr Richardson and Professor Sayles—have pressed their arguments a great deal farther than Maitland was prepared to do. Text and introduction of the *Memoranda de Parliamento* both make clear that the redressing of grievances, sometimes by judicial means, was one function—and no doubt a very important function—of Edward I's parliaments. But that is a different thing from saying that it was *the* function of these early parliaments—"When we have stripped every non-essential away," Messrs Richardson and Sayles put it, "the essence of them is the dispensing of justice by the king or by someone who in a very special sense represents the king."[1] It is by no means certain that Maitland would have agreed with them.

That Maitland, editing what began as a volume of petitions, should have as his principal concern the petitory and judicial element in parliament was natural enough. But that element cannot properly be made the *essential* of the early parliament unless, in some way or another, it is possible to establish a relationship between that sort of business and the summons of representatives. For, though it is very well to say that there is no constitutional importance to be attached to the presence of the commons in parliament before 1327,[2] the fact remains that Edward I repeatedly thought it worth while to summon them, and no doubt had some good reason for making it *parliament* to which he brought his representatives. One explanation of why he did this, which, had it proved acceptable to historians, would have provided the necessary link between petitions and representation, had been put forward some ten years before the *Memoranda de Parliamento* appeared. In 1885 Ludwig Riess had published his *Geschichte des Wahlrechts zum englischen Parlament im Mittelalter*, with its attractive thesis that the function of the representatives was to bring petitions of grievances to parliament and, in due course, to carry back to their "constituencies" the council's replies. This book was, of course, well known to

[1] "The Early Records of the English Parliaments", *B.I.H.R.*, v (1927–8), 133.
[2] G. O. Sayles, *The Medieval Foundations of England*, p. 456.

Maitland (his copy of it, indeed, is in the Cambridge University Library), and its central argument undoubtedly attracted him, though in the introduction to the *Memoranda* he approached it with some caution—

> The doctrine that in these days the representatives of the shires and towns were called to parliament not in order that they might act in concert on behalf of the commons of England, but in order that each might represent before the king in council the grievances and the interests of the particular community, county or borough, that sent him thither, may easily be pressed too far, but we shall probably think that there is no little truth in it if we ask what the knights and burgesses were doing while the king and his councillors were slowly disposing of this great mass of petitions, many of which were presented by shires and boroughs.[1]

Unfortunately this thesis of the connection between representation and petitory business does not stand up to examination. It was demolished by Professor G. L. Haskins, who showed, for instance, that in Maitland's own parliament of 1305 only 9 per cent of the petitions were from shires and towns as against 16 per cent from other groups, 51 per cent from individuals and 24 per cent from religious communities.[2]

Because of this failure to discover a firm connection between the judicial activities of parliaments and the summons to them of representatives, as well as for other reasons, recent writers have reacted away from the conciliar and judicial interpretation, laying their stress once again on fiscal, and even political, considerations, and reverting to something like the other idea of a full parliament—"an assembly", Professor Wilkinson says, "in which contemporaries could see reflected not the king's council but, in some sense, the *universitas regni*, the assembled power and majesty of the realm".[3] It is, moreover, the omnicompetence of such an assembly that is emphasized. Such an approach may seem to leave on one side those aspects of early parliamentary development that

[1] *M. de P.*, p. lxxv.

[2] Haskins, "The Petitions of Representatives in the Parliaments of Edward I", *E.H.R.*, liii (1938), p. 8.

[3] B. Wilkinson, *Studies in the Constitutional History of the Thirteenth and Fourteenth Centuries* (1937), p. 14.

most interested Maitland—or at least those that he happened to study. In one very important sense, however, historians of this sort are nearer to Maitland than are Mr Richardson and Professor Sayles. Like Maitland, they envisage parliament as developing and yet still incomplete: they do not regard it as a fixed and established institution at the outset of Edward I's reign.

VII

THE YEAR BOOKS

In the development of the English common law the existence of a tradition of case reporting has been of crucial importance. If the prehistory of that tradition can be said, in a sort of way, to have started with Bracton, its real history had its beginnings early in the reign of Edward I, with the commencement of the Year Books. "This surely is a memorable event," Maitland wrote; "when duly considered it appears as one of the great events of English history. Today men are reporting at Edinburgh and Dublin, at Boston and San Francisco, at Quebec and Sydney and Cape Town, at Calcutta and Madras. Their pedigree is unbroken and indisputable. It goes back to some nameless lawyers at Westminster to whom a happy thought had come."[1] To the immediate successors of those first reporters, and to the Year Books that, in the reign of Edward II, they produced, Maitland was to give much of the precious last five or six years of his life.

Some of the long series of Year Books had found their way into print in the black-letter editions of the sixteenth and seventeenth centuries, and on them some of the most erudite lawyers had based their learning, like that Serjeant Maynard who used to read them in his coach: the 1678 edition associated with Maynard was, however, edited rather feebly. In 1800 the Select Committee on the Public Records recommended that those available only in manuscript should be published and the old black-letter editions reprinted.[2] From 1863 the first half of this recommendation began to be implemented with the publication in the Rolls Series

[1] *Year Books, 1 & 2 Edward II*, Selden Soc., vol. 17, p. xv.
[2] *Reports from the Select Committee appointed to inquire into the State of the Public Records*, 1800, p. 16.

of a number of Year Books of the reigns of Edward I and Edward III.[1] Then in 1886 there came a scheme for republication of the old printed Year Books by one or more of the Inns of Court with financial assistance from the Treasury. On 24 April of that year Maitland, whose opinion had been sought a few days earlier, wrote a long letter to Maxwell-Lyte on the subject of a new edition. What he thought was necessary was a good text, based on comparison of the black-letter books with all available manuscripts, and accompanied by an English translation. Each volume should have an index, and for each reign, or period of twenty years, there should be a more elaborate digest. Though there should be a small supervisory committee, one man must initially do the job—"I do not think that a committee can make a text or a translation"—and Maitland would much have liked to be he. "When we met", he wrote to Maxwell-Lyte, "you were good enough to say that conceivably I might be asked to take a part in the work. This I should regard as a very high honour and therefore you may permit me to say what I have to offer. I consider that the readership I hold in Cambridge ought to require of me about half my working time. The other half I would very willingly devote to work on the Year Books."[2]

The plan failed to materialize, but perhaps his experience in using the Year Books for his paper on Malice Aforethought in 1883, coupled with his inquiries made in connection with the 1886 proposal, led to the outburst in his inaugural lecture as Downing Professor—"Look at the hopeless mass of corruption that passes as a text of the Year Books."[3] Later, in connection with the *History of English Law*, he came to realize that a tolerable edition of the Year Books was an indispensable preliminary to the production of a legal history of the later Middle Ages.[4] Indeed, Sir William Holdsworth went so far as to say that it was Maitland's refusal to be satisfied with any but the very best evidence that led him to turn to work on the Year Books instead of continuing the *History of English Law* beyond the reign of

[1] *20 & 21, 30 & 31, 32 & 33 Edward I; 12–20 Edward III.*
[2] *Letters*, p. 21.   [3] *C.P.*, i, 484.
[4] *H.E.L.*, i, p. xxxv.

Henry III.[1] Whatever truth there may be in that, towards the last years of the century Maitland's mind turned more and more to the problem of the Year Books. He had a great admiration for L. O. Pike, who was editing some of them for the Rolls Series, and in 1897 expressed the wish that that scholar might be freed from all other duties, training two or three assistant editors, and turning out two volumes a year.[2]

That being his attitude, it was natural that, with the Selden Society well launched, he should seek to direct its efforts towards the publication of the Year Books, and, when he had done that, to undertake much of the necessary work himself. "Then there are the Year Books," he wrote to Poole on 30 July 1901, "and I have talked so much about the need for a new edition that I am bound to give them the best of my time now that the Selden has taken the matter up."[3] The next year—exactly as he had envisaged for Pike five years previous—he was seeking assistance. "We may be at the beginning of a very big affair," he told Poole, "but the project will fail if I have to tackle it single handed." More specifically he said in the same letter that there might be a prospect for a young man who could afford to wait[4]—a phrase that gives an ironic twist to his later approach to A. F. Pollard, for waiting was exactly what Pollard was not prepared to do. The circumstances of the negotiation were amusingly typical of the two men. In the spring of 1903, Pollard, seeking election to the Chair of Constitutional History at University College, London, approached Maitland, although he was not, in fact, acquainted with him, for a testimonial. Maitland giving the testimonial, no doubt on the strength of what he knew of Pollard's work, accompanied it with a suggestion that Pollard might assist in the Year Book project. To this he received a categorical refusal, Pollard rather impertinently suggesting amongst other possible assistants G. J. Turner,[5] whom Maitland,

[1] Holdsworth, *The Historians of Anglo-American Law*, p. 141.

[2] *E.H.R.*, xii (1897), 350.   [3] *Letters*, p. 230.

[4] 22 April 1902, *ibid.*, pp. 242–243.

[5] 29 Apr. 1903, Pollard to Maitland; 1 May 1903, Pollard to Maitland, C.U. Add. MS. 7007.

as a matter of fact, had known for a number of years—indeed, his hand writing is on the galley proofs of Turner's ill-fated *Brevia Placitata*, set up in 1897 but not reaching publication until over half a century later.[1]

Yet in the upshot it was Turner who did become Maitland's assistant, giving him some help with the first two volumes published by the Selden Society in the Year Book series, and so much with the third volume that Maitland wished to put his name on the title-page as joint editor; the fourth volume Turner completed after Maitland's death.[2] In some ways the two must have been an oddly assorted couple. Maitland, for all his preternatural accuracy, worked exceedingly fast: Turner was painstaking, slow and perfectionist. Moreover, this difference reflected a deeper divergence in their work. "If Maitland's work leaves the impression of light coming in a sudden flash of intuition," Professor Plucknett puts it, "Turner's seems to show the almost imperceptible dawn breaking after a long night of contemplation."[3] Yet the association was happy and productive.

By that time a very sick man, condemned to winter in the Canaries—"abjuring the realm", he called it—Maitland carried his editorial work (and, on at least one occasion, his assistant) with him. His dogged persistence with this labour was markedly courageous, though his references to it in his correspondence were sufficiently light-hearted. "I am beginning to think that, even if I vanish from the scene," he said in a letter to Fisher on 10 January 1904, "not only vol. 2 but also vol. 3 of the Year Books will be published. . . . It is not exciting work—not half so grand as writing of Tudors and Boney—but it seems the best that I can do nowadays and will bring a little money to me, my exs, ads. or assns, even when photographs are paid for."[4]

In the meanwhile, as if Maitland had not enough Year Book troubles on his hands—the problem of financing publication, the essential difficulty of the material, the uncertainty of how long

[1] *Brevia Placitata*, Selden Soc., vol. 66, p. vii.
[2] See P. H. Winfield's Memoir of Turner in Selden Soc., vol. 63.
[3] *Brevia Placitata*, p. viii.
[4] *Letters*, p. 291.

his own precarious health would let him continue as editor—in the summer of 1902, when his first volume was well advanced, there was added a further embarrassment. The matter was perhaps never much more than an annoyance, and in the upshot of no great importance, but it is interesting as one of the few occasions when Maitland, the most peaceable of men, came near to crossing swords with some of his American colleagues. On 10 August C. C. Soule, who, the previous year, had published a paper on Year Book bibliography,[1] wrote him a rather pompous letter, outlining a most ambitious scheme for publication. Maitland was put out by this project—rightly, since it had been worked out behind his back and appeared to envisage interference with the Selden Society's own plans.[2] Although six months later Pike wrote reassuringly that no such interference with Maitland's period was, in fact, contemplated,[3] on 1 March 1903 Maitland sent Soule a stiff letter. While, he wrote, it was not for him to say what the council of the Selden Society might do, he thought it unlikely that a proposal to alter the shape of the society's books would be accepted, nor would the council want to be pledged to complete the Edward II Year Books within a given time—surely a suggestion of American pressure and hustle on the latter point. "I think it far better", Maitland concluded, "that we should go our several ways: that is to say the Seld. Soc. on the one side and you and your associates on the other. And of course you will understand that the Society, even if it had the will, has not the power to prevent you from including the books of Edw. II in your scheme. Thus I fear that I must ask you to withdraw my name, etc." The tone is, for Maitland, untypically severe, and equally significant is the fact that this was one of the very few letters of which he seems to have troubled to make, and keep, a copy.[4] Few scholars on either side of the Atlantic will regret his decision to continue along his own lines.

[1] *Harvard Law Review*, xiv.

[2] 10 Aug. 1902, Soule to Maitland, C.U. Add. MS. 7006; see also letters from Pollock and Lock to Maitland, *ibid.*

[3] 18 Feb. 1903, Pike to Maitland, C.U. Add. MS. 7007.

[4] *Letters*, p. 275.

To the task of editing the Year Books Maitland brought
nearly twenty years of experience in transcribing and editing
medieval legal manuscripts of very various kinds, and—perhaps
just as important—he brought, too, that practical common sense
that characterized all his work as an editor. As always, he began
by determining what was essential, and then, preferring the
substance to the shadow, set about achieving it in the simplest
possible way. So with the Year Books of Edward II, having made
up his mind that the seventeenth-century text was "too bad to be
understood, and therefore too bad to be tolerated",[1] and that it
was impossible to make a satisfactory translation from the old
printed text,[2] he set about making a French text. His method of
doing this, however, was a good deal less ambitious than that
employed by Pike in his editions of the Year Books of the
succeeding reign. Maitland did not attempt a full-scale collation
and to give a translation in strict agreement with the text:
materials for his translation have sometimes to be sought in his
notes. This system is no doubt open to theoretical objections
from the purist point of view. On the other hand, it must always
be remembered that, for the reign of Edward II, Maitland was
faced by a large number of manuscripts, containing so many
versions as to make formal collation neither meaningful nor
indeed possible.[3] It should not, in any event, be represented that
Maitland's editing was slipshod or that he was seeking un-
justifiably to cut his corners. No one who pays regard to the
infinite pains he took over Year Book French could believe that.
"So I have been copying Year Books from the manuscripts that I
brought from Cambridge," he wrote Leslie Stephen from the
Canaries in December 1901, "and since the scribes did not finish
their words and I have to supply the endings I have been com-
pelled to take a serious interest in old French Grammar."[4] More-

---

[1] *Year Books, 1 & 2 Edward II*, Selden Soc., vol. 17, p. xxviii.

[2] *ibid.*, p. xxiii.

[3] There are good discussions in Pike, *Year Book, 20 Edward III*, ii, pp.
xxii–xxiii, and Plucknett, *Year Books of Richard II, 13 Richard II*, pp. xxii–
xxiii.

[4] *Letters*, p. 237.

over, very much on Pike's lines, he compared his Year Book cases with the corresponding records, ascertaining the correct names of counsel from the plea rolls and so on; and like Pike, he included references to Fitzherbert's Abridgement.

The objection to Maitland's work on the Year Books, so far from being that he took his editorial task too lightly, is indeed quite the reverse—that it consumed too much of the short time that remained to him. This was no doubt what A. L. Smith meant when he confessed to almost grudging so much brilliant work wasted on some of his material—"it is like finding an electric light kept on in a cellar".[1] Maitland himself admitted to Fisher in 1905 that "life is so short and these Year Books run away with a devil of a lot of time".[2]

Yet quite apart from its value in its own right, without that close work Maitland could never have written the brilliant introductions to his three Year Book volumes that, quite rightly, brought him the Ames Prize of the Harvard Law School.[3] The first of these, to the Year Book of 1 and 2 Edward II, was especially interesting. In it Maitland examined the origins and purpose of the Year Books, rejecting Plowden's hearsay evidence that they were the work of official reporters, which lack of record of appointments and subsequent payment rendered unlikely; rather he thought that they were made "by learners for learners".[4] With the sense of "belonging" that marked so much of his most persuasive writing, he celebrated the achievement of the medieval common lawyers and described in memorable phrases the sort of men they were—

No, the clergy were not the only learned men in England, the only cultivated men, the only men of ideas. Vigorous intellectual effort was to be found outside the monasteries and the universities. These lawyers are worldly men, not men of sterile caste; they marry and found families, some of which become as noble as any

[1] Smith, *Frederic William Maitland*, p. 39.
[2] 5 Mar. 1905, *Letters*, p. 334.
[3] *L.Q.R.*, xxiii (1907), 139.
[4] *Year Books, 1 & 2 Edward II*, Selden Soc., vol. 17, p. xiii; *Year Books, 3 Edward II*, Selden Soc., vol. 20, p. xii.

in the land; but they are in their way learned, cultivated men,
linguists, logicians, tenacious disputants, true lovers of the nice
case and the moot-point. They are gregarious, clubable men,
grouping themselves in hospices, which become schools of law,
multiplying manuscripts, arguing, learning and teaching, the great
mediators between life and logic, a reasoning, reasonable element
in the English nation.[1]

Technically the most remarkable feature of this first introduction was Maitland's fifty-page disquisition on the grammar,
syntax and philology of the Anglo-Norman French in which the
Year Books were written.[2] This was a *tour de force* of inductive
reasoning. Just as five or six years previously, in the quiet of
Horsepools, he had patiently counted Domesday hides and made
his statistical calculations about them, so in the Canaries in 1902
he went to work on the linguistic complexities that he felt must
be faced by a Year Book editor. No scholarship could have
involved more literally original research, for secondary authorities
to aid him were almost entirely lacking. Nor could anything be
more typical of the flexibility of Maitland's mind and the way he
came to apply it to a new subject. With him the matter was often
not so much a preconceived notion that this or that subject was a
desirable topic for research, scarcely was it a matter of free choice:
issues arose in the course of his work that, to the best of his ability,
had to be resolved. Such were the grammar, syntax and philology
of the language of the Year Book compilers. What Maitland
wrote about them met with the warm approval of linguistic
scholars like Meyer,[3] and the editors of the *Cambridge History of
English Literature* reprinted it under the title "The Anglo-French
Law Language". Critical assessments of this piece of work, and
attempts to correct and bring it up to date, have more recently
been put forward by Miss Dominica Legge[4] and Mr J. P. Collas.[5]
According to the latter, while Maitland's description of the
spelling and morphology, and of much of the syntactical

[1] *Year Books, 1 & 2 Edward II*, Selden Soc., vol. 17, pp. lxxx–lxxxi.
[2] *ibid.*, pp. xxxiii–lxxxi.
[3] *L.Q.R.*, xxiii (1907), 142.
[4] *Year Book, 10 Edward II*, Selden Soc., vol. 54, pp. xxx–xlii.
[5] *Year Book, 12 Edward II*, Selden Soc., vol. 65, pp. xii–lxiv.

peculiarity of Year Book language has remained authoritative, his fragmentary treatment of their vocabulary is ultimately misleading.[1]

About the introductions to the second and third volumes it is necessary to say less.

That to the second volume was, for particular reasons, of unusual brevity. The opening volume of the series had been received with so much enthusiasm that one member of the council of the Selden Society, Stuart Moore, suggested dropping all other publications in favour of more rapid printing of the Year Books.[2] That, of course, could not be done; but, in response to the interest aroused, the production of the second in the series was speeded up, and it was issued to members as an extra, bonus volume for 1904. In these circumstances want of time and space put a long introduction out of the question. Maitland did, however, include some interesting remarks about the origins of law reporting, referring to one of his manuscripts that contained a few cases probably from the first decade of Edward I's reign—"cases", he said with some awe, "decided by men who were on the bench in Henry III's day and who must have known Bracton".[3]

Brevity was not a characteristic of the introduction to the third volume, which Maitland described to Fisher as "a long and dull affair about the manuscripts".[4] After a few opening pages of generalization, in which he reiterated his belief that the Year Books that he was handling were students' note-books, Maitland did indeed turn to a minute consideration of the manuscripts that he and Turner had used. His discussion of them was valuable; but it must have put the enthusiasm of members of the Selden Society to the test, and certainly it defies any attempt at summary.

"It will one day seem a wonderful thing", Maitland wrote in the preface to his first Year Book volume, "that men once thought

---

[1] *ibid.*, p. xvii.
[2] 11 Dec. 1903, Lock to Maitland, C.U. Add. MS. 7007.
[3] *Year Books, 2 & 3 Edward II*, Selden Soc., vol. 19, p.x.
[4] 5 Mar. 1905, *Letters*, p. 334.

M.–H

that they could write the history of medieval England without using the Year Books."[1] Although the optimistically conceived plans of 1886 and of Soule a dozen years later have not been implemented, at least Maitland's example has been followed by others—the Selden Society has a dozen Year Book volumes to its credit, the Ames Foundation a further three. Has the effort put into this work been worth while, either from the point of view of the specifically legal historian or of the general medieval English historian? Forty years ago Mr H. G. Richardson, in the sort of iconoclastic article that he has always written so well, expressed some doubts. To him it seemed that the plea rolls rivalled the Year Books in the intimate picture that they gave of the law courts, while he argued that, for social and political history, the material they provided was infinitely more varied and detailed—especially since the concentration of Year Book reporting mainly on the common pleas meant that king's bench cases, often of wider significance, escaped it. To those thinking like Mr Richardson, then, overstress on publication of Year Books at the expense of getting original records into print was a matter for regret,[2] and it is true that, emphasizing as they do unusual pleadings or unusual points of law, the Year Books have less general value to the historian than the plea rolls.

We must, of course, be careful how far we make Maitland responsible for any such tendency. Few historians have had a greater respect for the original record than he, and the dichotomy, Year Books–plea rolls, would not to him have seemed meaningful. As early as 1888 he told Ames that he would willingly try to trace any case he wanted from the Year Books to the rolls—"I enjoy a good hunt." "Whenever the happy day comes", he went on, "when the Year Books are reprinted the records will have to be used."[3] He warmly approved of Pike's use of the plea rolls to shed extra light on the Year Book text, and this was something that he was careful to do in those that he later

[1] *Year Books, 1 & 2 Edward II*, Selden Soc., vol. 17, p. xx.

[2] "Year Books and Plea Rolls as Sources of Historical Information", *T.R.H.S.*, 4th series (1922).

[3] 6 May 1888, *Letters*, p. 41.

edited.[1] Nor was he unaware of the inferiority of Year Book to plea-roll evidence even in some fields of purely legal history. For instance in 1888, when, in his paper "The Beatitude of Seisin", he was attempting to trace the change that came over the concept of seisin in the later Middle Ages, he pointed out the necessity of relying on the Year Books. "It may be well therefore", he added, "to observe that the Year Books are for this or any similar purpose very unsatisfactory material, because they are chiefly concerned with points of pleading, and by the middle of the fourteenth century pleadings had become very unreal things. . . . A good selection from the Plea Rolls would be much better material."[2] Yet the cut and thrust of counsels' argument, the full rigour of the forensic game, had infinite appeal to Maitland. If Sir Charles Ogilvie's contention that Maitland admired common-law technique and technicality too much[3] has any validity, it is in the context of his Year Book studies. "The play of reasoning among the counsel at the bar", he admitted openly, "is much more interesting than any series of decided points could be."[4] That was clearly true for Maitland, and it is probably true for many others of us; but "more interesting" is not necessarily synonymous with "more important". The record must always be superior to the report.

[1] See *Year Books, 1 & 2 Edward II*, Selden Soc., vol. 17, p. xxxi; *Year Books, 3 Edward II*, Selden Soc., vol. 20, p. liv—"a report that has not been compared with the parallel record is often treacherous ground"; *R.C.L.*, p. 148—". . . certain discussions in the Year Books, which have never, I believe, been fully explained because they have never been compared with the plea rolls."

[2] *C.P.*, i, 434–435.

[3] See above, p. 10. Note, however, *Year Books, 3 Edward II*, Selden Soc., vol. 20, p. xi—"We may indeed suppose that to a young man of this time the law that the justices and serjeants discussed did not seem quite so technical, quite so arbitrary, as it appears to us. He could see the social and economic import of rules which we are tempted to regard as perverse displays of ingenuity."

[4] *Year Books, 2 & 3 Edward II*, Selden Soc., vol. 19, p. xiv.

VIII

CANON LAW IN THE MEDIEVAL
ENGLISH CHURCH

NOT the least interesting feature of Maitland's scholarship is the means by which he came to study the widely different topics on which he wrote. His work was never channelled in a single groove or pointed to a single end; he had a lively, flexible mind that was always ready to follow a hint from the data that it happened to be processing. In particular, if he became suspicious of the validity of any piece of received and traditionally accepted learning, he was not content until he had subjected the whole matter to his own critical investigation, stating his conclusions, if they differed from those generally held, with an admirable mixture of modesty and courage. So it was with his studies on the canon law—"a raid into unfamiliar country", as Professor Plucknett has called them.[1] The view that he came to query—that the medieval English church never held as authoritative the whole body of the Roman canon law—enjoyed support in two quite separate quarters: on the one hand, it had behind it a three-hundred-year-old common-law tradition and, on the other—perhaps to be taken more seriously—it had recently received Stubbs's unqualified blessing.

The common-law teaching in this connection derived from the sixteenth-century doctrine of royal supremacy over the church and the attempt artificially to project that supremacy backwards into pre-Reformation times. The term "the old Canons", used in the Henrician Act for the Submission of the

---

[1] Plucknett, "Execrabilis in the Commons Pleas: Further Studies", *Cambridge Law Journal*, i (1921), 60.

Clergy, referred to Lyndwood's *Provinciale*,[1] and it was assumed that the provincial constitutions, as they appeared in that collection, contained the whole older law of the English church.[2] These were what Coke meant when he spoke of "the king's lawes Ecclesiasticall", and, as the argument was developed, it followed that only such portions of the Roman canon law as had been formally received enjoyed authority in the medieval English church. Even Edmund Gibson, whose admirable *Codex Juris Ecclesiastici Anglicani* enjoyed the advantage of standing a little outside the common-law tradition, was ambivalent on this topic, in one context stating quite correctly that, where no rule was provided by our own domestic laws, the body of the canon law was received by the church, but arguing elsewhere that this obtained its sanction from the king.[3]

Of more direct relevance, the matter was the subject of learned pleading and judgments in Maitland's own century. In 1844 *Regina v. Millis*, which he described as "the stronghold of the opinion that I am questioning",[4] was a case that turned on the validity of a marriage performed in Ireland by a Presbyterian minister at which no Anglican clergyman was present: one of its central issues was whether the Roman canon law principle that a marriage could be valid without a priest was applicable. On a divided opinion in the Irish Court of King's Bench, the matter came to the House of Lords. To the Lords, Lord Chief Justice Tindal reported the opinion of the English common-law judges that the law by which, from the earliest times, the spiritual courts had been regulated was not the general canon law but a law modified by provincial constitutions as well as by parliament. Three out of the six law lords accepted the argument, taking the line that they were dealing with a Roman canon that the medieval English church had never received.[5] The same line was taken,

[1] J. V. Bullard and H. C. Bell, *Lyndwood's Provinciale* (1929), p. 1.

[2] H. W. C. Davis, "The Canon Law in England", *Zeitschrift der Savigny-Stiftung für Rechtsgeschichte*, 1913, p. 356.

[3] E. Gibson, *Codex Juris Ecclesiastici Anglicani*, pp. xxviii and viii.

[4] Maitland, "William Lyndwood", *E.H.R.*, xi (1896), 447.

[5] *The English Reports*, VIII (Clark and Finnelly), pp. 844–982. Lord

and the point even more definitively put, in Sir Robert Philli-more's judgment in *Martin v. Mackonochie*, 1868. That judgment is worth quoting at some length as indicative of the received learning of the common lawyers in the years just before Maitland wrote—

> The rules of the general Canon Law were principally introduced into this country, and considerably modified in their introduction, through the medium of provincial constitutions passed by the authority of the metropolitans of England . . . England possesses in her provincial constitutions, collected by Lyndewode, a body of domestic ecclesiastical law, upon which, before the Reformation, a national character was in many respects impressed. The common law was always disposed to recognize these constitutions, while to the general Canon Law it always manifested considerable averse-ness.[1]

Such was the legal view of the status of canon law in the medieval English church. The practising lawyer's attitude to history is sometimes oddly irresponsible, as Stubbs was to dis-cover when, in 1881, Gladstone appointed him to the Royal Commission on Ecclesiastical Courts. Yet, great though his differences with his legal colleagues on the commission were, on the crucial matter of the general canon law's lack of authority his position did not differ from theirs—indeed, in the historical appendices that he wrote for the commission's report he sought to justify the common-law doctrine. "Attempts to force on the church and nation the complete canon law of the middle ages", he wrote, "were always unsuccessful"; or again, after speaking of Gratian's Decretum, Gregory IX's Decretals, Boniface VIII's

---

Brougham did not, to his credit, accept the argument. "All Europe, including England," he said, "lived under the same religion, under the same ecclesiastical system, under the same spiritual rule" (p. 722).

[1] *The Law Reports, High Court of Admiralty and Ecclesiastical Courts*, ii, 153. Against the received view see Sir John Stoddart, *A letter to the Right Honourable the Lord Brougham and Vaux on the Opinions of the Judges in the Irish Marriage Case*, 1844; *Observations on the Opinion delivered by the Right Honourable the Lord Cottenham on the Writ of Error in the Case of the Queen v. Millis*, 1844. See also the case of Beamish v. Beamish, *The English Reports*, xi, 735–769. Both authorities are cited by Maitland, *H.E.L.*, ii, 372 note.

Sexts, the Clementines and Extravagants, "A knowledge of these", he said, "was the scientific equipment of the ecclesiastical jurist, but the texts were not authoritative." Moreover, though this was scarcely the fault of Stubbs, his thesis was used by the High Church party as an argument for the Church of England's continuity and for the playing down of the revolutionary character of the Reformation. As Maitland put it, they maintained that the Church of England had been Protestant before the Reformation and Catholic afterwards.[1]

About this view of the limited authority of the canon law in medieval England it is probable that Maitland very early began to have doubts, for he seems to have said in his constitutional history lectures, first given in 1887, that the English church was but a branch or member of the Roman church and that its provincial convocations were not supreme over it.[2] Nevertheless, as was so frequently the case in his scholarship, it was study on a point of detail that really set him questioning the accepted thesis. He himself tells us in the preface to his *Roman Canon Law in the Church of England* how his chapter on marriage in the *History of English Law* forced him to make an incursion into ecclesiastical jurisprudence.[3] The effect of an unprejudiced study of the attitude of thirteenth-century English churchmen to marriage questions was to bring him to an unfashionable and unorthodox conclusion—that the authority of the Roman canon law over the English church courts was complete:

> We have the clearest proof [he wrote] that at that time the law of the catholic and Roman church was being enforced in England. We have this not only in the decretal of Alexander III . . . but also in the many appeals about matrimonial matters that were being taken from England to Rome. It would have been as impossible for the courts Christian of this country to maintain about this vital point a schismatical law of their own as it would now be for a judge of the High Court to persistently disregard the decisions of the House of Lords: there would have been an appeal from every sentence, and reversal would have been a matter of

[1] *Essays*, p. xxi.
[2] *C.H.*, p. 507.
[3] *R.C.L.*, p. 5.

course. And then, had this state of things existed even for a few years, surely some English prelate or canonist would have been at pains to state our insular law. No one did anything of the kind. To say that the English church received or adopted the catholic law of marriage would be untrue; her rulers never conceived that they were free to pick and choose their law.[1]

His conclusions in the one matter of marriage, and the impression they had left in his mind, led him to further inquiries of a more general character. "I ought to have been writing lectures about the history of the Canon Law", he wrote to Poole in the Long Vacation of 1895. "Instead of so doing I have been led away into a lengthy discourse on Lyndwood. I have come to a result that seems to be heterodox."[2]

The paper on Lyndwood, together with two others, entitled "Church, State, and Decretals" and "William of Drogheda and the Universal Ordinary", appeared in the *English Historical Review* in 1896–1897. The year following, along with three minor essays, they were brought together as a volume under the title *Roman Canon Law in the Church of England*. In the preface to that book Maitland expressed the hope that, in their new version, they were somewhat improved;[3] but, in fact, the alterations in the principal papers were minimal. In the second of them, the final sentence, as it had appeared in the *English Historical Review*, was cut out in the book—perhaps because, even by Maitland's standards, it was too self-depreciatory; one of the early paragraphs of "William of Drogheda" received a little expansion. For the rest, the changes in text were no more than very occasional verbal corrections. Four or five footnotes were omitted, an odd one added, and perhaps a couple slightly amended.

The theme of the three main essays was really identical—the acknowledged superiority in the medieval English church of the Roman canon law.[4]

---

[1] *H.E.L.*, ii, 373.   [2] 15 Aug. 1895, *Letters*, p. 143.
[3] *R.C.L.*, p. vi.
[4] In *H.E.L.*, i, 113, he spoke of Englishmen in Italy taking part in the

The first dealt with William Lyndwood, in the earlier half of the fifteenth century principal official to the Archbishop of Canterbury and author in 1430 of the *Provinciale*, the main English authority on late-medieval canon law; to his critical examination of Lyndwood's work Maitland added some evidence from John of Ayton, the glossator (*c.* 1340) of the legatine constitutions. In the course of this study Maitland marshalled a whole series of arguments against the thesis of English ecclesiastical independence in the Middle Ages—the absence of native canonists, following an independent, "national" line was, he thought, notable; he found no tendency in his sources to doubt the Pope's legislative power or the binding force of decretals— indeed, anyone calling a decretal in question was reckoned a heretic; Lyndwood, he demonstrated, was firmly on the Pope's side against the general council; as to local canon law, he showed that legative statutes were reckoned superior to provincial, that the latter were few in number, and discrepancy between them and the general canon law rare, since they seem rather to have been envisaged as by-laws operating within the framework of the *ius commune* than as legislation standing in its own right.[1]

The central argument of Maitland's second paper was that two very different propositions had tended to be confused, alike by judges and by historians—(*a*) that in England the state did not allow the church to appropriate certain considerable portions of the wide field of jurisdiction that the canonists claimed, and (*b*) that the courts Christian in England held themselves free to reject canon law. The first of these is manifestly true, and, of course, Maitland accepted it, showing in his examination of the thesis how a bargain was struck between church and state. In two ways he felt that this operated to the church's advantage—its

---

making of the *Compilationes Antiquae*. But he does not seem to have been aware of the distinguished late twelfth-century canonists, Bartholomew of Exeter, Roger of Worcester, Richard of Canterbury, and Baldwin, abbot of Ford. For them see Charles Duggan, *Twelfth Century Decretal Collections and their importance in English History* (1963), p. 118.

[1] For one example of the custom of the church in England departing from the *ius commune* see *H.E.L.*, i, 613.

excommunication was enforced by the secular courts, and it was left an exclusive jurisdiction over testamentary causes. On the other hand, he reckoned that the church suffered disadvantages from the agreement, too—the *privilegium fori* was confined within narrow bounds: from Edward I's time the royal justices traversed the assertion that in personal actions clerks enjoy the *privilegium fori*, maintaining that they enjoyed it in cases of felony only; again, another feature of the agreement was that secular justice kept tight control of ecclesiastical patronage: Alexander III's decretal to Henry II claimed causes dealing with patronage for the church courts, but Maitland argued that this was countered by writs of prohibition, and he saw Henry's assertion that advowsons were outside the scope of the courts Christian as the foundation of all subsequent legislation against provisors. The second proposition, the notion that the English church courts felt themselves entitled to reject canon law as it suited them, Maitland—and this is what was important for his general theme —showed to be false. However much the barons at Merton in 1235 might say "Nolumus leges Angliae mutari", in the courts Christian the old ecclesiastical rule about bastardy continued to be enforced.

Maitland's third essay centred on the book of William of Drogheda, a thirteenth-century ecclesiastical lawyer whom we have already had occasion to mention,[1] portions of whose work are found in manuscripts at Caius College, Cambridge, and elsewhere.[2] What struck Maitland about William was his steady assumption in this book for practitioners in the ecclesiastical courts that the most remunerative litigation will be cases brought in the first instance before a court constituted by a papal writ. At first sight it may appear odd that the initial step taken by an English litigant should so often be the impetration of a papal writ appointing judges delegate to hear his cause—why should he not start his case in the court of bishop or archdeacon? But Maitland showed that there were solid reasons that made it

[1] See above, p. 51.
[2] For the Caius College MSS. see M. R. James, *A Descriptive Catalogue of the Manuscripts in the Library of Gonville and Caius College*, i, pp. 47, 83–84.

advantageous to secure judges delegate right at the start—so common had appeals become that sooner or later the course would come before the Pope, and therefore, perhaps, the sooner the better; again, where co-defendants in a suit came from different dioceses, the bishop's court of neither was competent to try them both; perhaps most advantageous of all, the plaintiff who secured a writ from the Pope seems to have enjoyed some say in the choice of judges delegate. In any event, what Maitland stresses most of all is that William's recommendations are in harmony with the view his thirteenth-century contemporaries held as to the Pope's jurisdictional authority. "Drogheda", he says, "merely registers the fact that the pope is the universal 'ordinary'."[1]

It would be disappointingly uncharacteristic of Maitland's work if these essays had not stimulated later scholars to studies in the medieval English canon law, and strange if, in a number of connections, such studies had not extended our knowledge of some of the matters that Maitland discussed and, on occasion, led to a querying of some of his conclusions, however much his central thesis in *Roman Canon Law in the Church of England* has continued to meet with acceptance.

The relationship between the general canon law and provincial constitutions, which was Maitland's main preoccupation in the Lyndwood essay,[2] can today be examined in a good deal more detail in the light of the work done by Professor C. R. Cheney and others. From this it is apparent that, in the century following the appearance of Gratian's Decretum, local legislation did, to some extent, change its function and become more significant than it had been. According to Gratian provincial councils could not make law, though they might enjoin the observance of laws already made, and hence twelfth-century provincial constitutions tended to be merely repetitive of the Roman canon law. "Later local legislation", Professor Cheney has put it, however, "completes and glosses, rather than repeats the law of the Corpus

[1] *R.C.L.*, p. 116.
[2] *ibid.*, pp. 19–44.

Iuris."[1] In particular the assimilation of Roman canons to local custom became one of the tasks of the provincial constitution.[2] Further down the ecclesiastical hierarchy, diocesan statutes had similar functions—they were used both for the publication of canons of general and provincial councils and for the reconciliation of custom and the general canon law.[3] Yet it is abundantly clear that local legislation of any sort, and at any level, never stood in its own right or enjoyed independence of the Roman canon law. Four times at least during the thirteenth century the Archbishop of Canterbury prefaced his canons with the statement that they were not introducing new law;[4] a diocesan statute, if it went against the *ius commune* of the church, was invalid.[5] In this connection, then, the position that Maitland took up has been proved by subsequent scholarship to be one that can be maintained.

The same cannot be claimed for all the arguments of his paper called "Church, State, and Decretals". Dealing as it did with the frontier area between the lay and spiritual jurisdictions, that paper's subject-matter has been re-examined by a number of scholars in the half-century since Maitland's death. At several points their work has made necessary some modifications of his findings.

The *privilegium fori*, which he was content to discuss in a very few pages,[6] has been made the subject of two full-length books.[7] While his description of the increasing restrictions placed on the privilege by the royal courts has been accepted, it has been pointed out that the growing inclusiveness of the term *clericus*

[1] C. R. Cheney, "Legislation of the Medieval English Church", *E.H.R.*, l (1935), 202.

[2] S. Kuttner, "Methodological Problems Concerning the History of the Canon Law", *Speculum*, XXX (1955), esp. p. 545.

[3] Cheney, *English Synodalia of the Thirteenth Century*, pp. 7 and 12.

[4] Cheney, *E.H.R.*, l (1935), 203.

[5] Cheney, *English Synodalia*, p. 10.

[6] *R.C.L.*, pp. 59–62. See, however, *H.E.L.*, i, 441–457, and "Henry II and the Criminous Clerks", *R.C.L.*

[7] R. Génestal, *Le Privilegium Fori en France* (1924); Gabel, *Benefit of Clergy*.

involved a wide extension of the range of persons who could claim benefit of clergy, so that from the end of the thirteenth century the numbers enjoying the privilege were very considerable indeed.[1]

To the question of jurisdiction on matters of ecclesiastical patronage, which Maitland also treated in this second paper,[2] a great deal of study has been applied.[3] From this it appears pretty conclusively that the courts Christian were much more active in this connection than Maitland realized. For the greater part of Henry II's reign, and perhaps longer, disputes about advowsons were frequently settled either by agreements made in the bishop's presence or by papal judges delegate.[4] Moreover, it has been pointed out that, to make effective the royal claim of jurisdiction put forward in c. 1 of the Constitutions of Clarendon, the prevention of suits between patrons in the church courts was not enough; control had also to be secured over suits between clerks that indirectly affected patrons' rights—and that is what some of the forms of prohibition cited by Glanvill were aiming to do.[5] Nevertheless, although, in the latter part of Henry II's reign, the decrees of the Lateran Council of 1179, on the one hand, and the royal writs of prohibition and darrein presentment, on the other, sharpened the issue,[6] the element of conflict between the two jurisdictions can be exaggerated—and perhaps was exaggerated by Maitland. It has been shown that the English church did not persistently oppose the royal courts' jurisdiction; nor were cases in the courts Christian stopped by the secular power until a writ of prohibition was sued out by the defendant[7]—

[1] Gabel, *op. cit.*, p. 62.

[2] *R.C.L.*, pp. 63–76.

[3] See especially G. B. Flahiff on prohibitions in *Mediaeval Studies* (Pontifical Institute of Mediaeval Studies, Toronto), iii, vi, vii, and J. W. Gray, "The Ius Presentandi in England from the Constitutions of Clarendon to Bracton", *E.H.R.*, lxvii (1952).

[4] *E.H.R.*, lxvii (1952), 564.

[5] Gray, *op. cit.*, pp. 485–486.

[6] Van Caenegem, *Royal Writs in England from the Conquest to Glanvill*, Selden Society, vol. 77.

[7] *B.I.H.R.*, xxv (1952), 21.

himself often a clerk.[1] As Professor Cheney has pointed out, there is a fundamental inconsistency in Maitland's account of the struggle over advowsons and the clergy's willingness to let such cases pass out of the sphere of the courts Christian.[2] Again, there were no doubt very many occasions where the bishop's admission and institution of a candidate for a benefice followed smoothly on his presentation by the patron; and even where it did not, and there was a dispute, this was generally resolved by a compromise, safeguarding both the patron's and the bishop's right.[3]

The most serious criticism of "Church, State, and Decretals", then, is that in it Maitland did overstress the extent to which the royal and ecclesiastical courts were in conflict. It was natural enough that he should do this, since, his purpose being to argue against the view that the church courts could reject the canon law, he wanted to distinguish their position from that of the royal courts which certainly could. Still, it was no doubt this element of exaggeration in Maitland's picture that made Sir Maurice Powicke give the warning that *Roman Canon Law in the Church of England* must be interpreted "in the light of the accommodation, as well as the disputes, between royal and ecclesiastical jurisdiction", and refer his readers to Prynne's *Exact Chronological Vindication of Our King's Supreme Ecclesiastical Jurisdiction on All Religious Affairs* as a sort of counterbalance to Maitland's book.[4]

It is, however, for the third of the essays, "William of Drogheda and the Universal Ordinary", that the sharpest attack seems to have been reserved. "Is it not a trait of a some-what unusual erudition", Maitland himself said, "that for an historical purpose Lyndwood has gone behind the Gregorian collection to the *Compilationes Prima et Tertia?*"[5] Certainly, at the time he was writing Maitland did not possess that erudition.

---

[1] Flahiff, *Mediaeval Studies*, iii (1941), p. 102.

[2] Cheney, *The English Church from Becket to Langton*, p. 110.

[3] Gray, *op. cit.*, p. 506.

[4] Powicke, *The Thirteenth Century* (Oxford History of England), p. 757.

[5] *R.C.L.*, p. 5.

In a sort of tailpiece to "William of Drogheda", where he discussed Alexander III's decretals to English bishops and judges delegate, he relied on those published by Gregory IX.[1] For this Mr Charles Duggan has recently taken him most severely to task.[2]

First, it is indisputable that the decretals as they appeared in the collections had lost much that would have been valuable to historians—notably, precision as to persons and places, dates and historical setting.[3] Of this Maitland was aware, and about it he wrote an amusing paragraph—

> Here, for example, is a missive which deals with a lawsuit between two English parsons. The parish of the one is variously designated as *Sander, Santer, Santen, Sandeia, Sandria, Sandinia, Sandeta, Sandaia, Fand, Sandola*; that of the other as *Pelen, Pele, Petel, Ploren., Pelin., Peleren., Pelerenen., Positione, Positioni, Pon., Porni, Peieren., Poinone, Portione, Pone, Portino, Porten, Potton*. Anyone who for his sins has endured the railway journey between Oxford and Cambridge will guess that the one village is Sandy, and the other Potton; but to the decretist the whereabouts of these places was less than nothing. They might be in Spain; they might be in Hungary; they might be nowhere.[4]

But what he did not know—or, if he knew it, was unable to do anything about—was that behind Gregory IX's Decretals, behind the *Compilationes Antiquae*, there were sources of a more reliable nature.

Again—and this was more serious—Maitland erred in thinking that the decretal collections represented Alexander's total issue, and that the proportions of them relating to particular districts indicated the proportions actually dispatched to each. On this basis he suggested that Alexander III's decretals sent to England amounted to more than a third of his issue to the whole church.[5] Today we know that this suggestion was mistaken, and

[1] *ibid.*, pp. 122–129.
[2] Duggan, *Twelfth Century Decretal Collections and their importance in English History*, esp. pp. 3–7, 140–141.
[3] *ibid.*, p. 62.
[4] *R.C.L.*, pp. 122–123.
[5] *ibid.*, p. 124.

that the predominance of "English" decretals in the collections
reflects a lively group of English canonists, preserving and bringing them together, rather than an especially high incidence of
decretals directed to England. It is in this connection that Mr
Duggan most sharply criticizes Maitland, speaking of him as
being "misled into a position which has vitiated most of the
later study of the subject" and of his having "grievously mis-
interpreted" the phenomena he studied.[1] It may be doubted how
realistic such criticism is. Mr Duggan's arguments, as he comes
near to admitting, depend on evidence that was not available
when Maitland wrote.[2] It was especially Stephan Kuttner's
Repertorium der Kanonistik (1140–1234), published in 1937, that
made possible a better understanding of the situation.[3]

About the three short papers that completed *Roman Canon Law
in the Church of England* it is necessary only to comment briefly.

"Henry II and the Criminous Clerks" rejected the view,
previously pretty generally held, that c. 3 of the Constitutions of
Clarendon meant that a clerk charged with a temporal offence
would be tried in the royal courts, and with an ecclesiastical
offence in the courts Christian, the king reserving to his court
the right to decide what offences are temporal and also asserting
the right to send delegates to view the doings of the church court.
Instead, Maitland held the scheme envisaged to be accusation in
the temporal court; trial, conviction and degradation in the
spiritual; and, finally, sentence in the temporal to the layman's
punishment. This essay originally appeared in the *English
Historical Review* as far back as 1892. At that time Maitland,
conscious that he was entering controversial ground, wrote to
Fisher about it, "I expect to be accursed by both parties."[4] In

---

[1] Duggan, *op. cit.*, p. 140.   [2] *ibid.*

[3] See G. Barraclough's review of Kuttner in *E.H.R.*, liii (1938); M. Cheney,
"The Compromise of Avranches of 1172 and the Spread of Canon Law in
England", *E.H.R.*, lvi (1941); Stephan Kuttner and Eleanor Rathbone,
"Anglo-Norman Canonists of the Twelfth Century", *Traditio*, vii (1949–51);
C. N. L. Brooke, "Canons of English Church Councils in the Early Decretal
Collections", *Traditio*, xiii (1957).

[4] 29 November 1891, Maitland to Fisher, *Letters*, p. 96.

fact, his interpretation has met with overwhelming acceptance. Very recently a secondary argument of this paper has, however, been challenged. Maitland considered that, on the text of the Decretum, Henry had an arguable case for what he was trying to do,[1] and that the canonical tradition was on his side. Mr Duggan, on the other hand, regarding the Decretum as conclusive in favour of neither of the parties, though he thinks it on balance favourable to Becket, argues that it is necessary to go to the canons themselves and their historical background: these, he feels, justify Becket and demand a reversal of Maitland's judgment.[2]

" 'Execrabilis' in the Common Pleas", first published in the *Law Quarterly Review* for 1896, was little more than a note, and it has small importance except as an example of the kind of legal conundrum that from time to time exercised Maitland. The real place of the episode in the conflict of jurisdiction over questions of plenarty or voidance of benefices is better studied in what Professor Plucknett has written about it than in Maitland's essay.[3] "The Deacon and the Jewess", written for the *Law Quarterly Review* in 1886 must be rated one of Maitland's most charming occasional papers: it was a sound instinct that led him to make it the tailpiece to his book, and a sound instinct, too, that caused Fisher, reprinting it yet again in the *Collected Papers*, to asterisk it as one of Maitland's pieces of most interest to the general reader.

Maitland's canon law studies amounted to a frontal attack on the orthodox opinion, and specifically on the position taken up by Stubbs in his appendices to the *Report of the Royal Commission on Ecclesiastical Courts*. That this was going to be the case, indeed, he became aware as early as September 1895, when he wrote to Poole, "I think it not impossible that what I say will irritate some good folk, though I hope to stick close to the legal

[1] *R.C.L.*, p. 143.

[2] Duggan, "The Becket Dispute and Criminous Clerks", *B.I.H.R.*, xxxv (1962).

[3] Plucknett, "Execrabilis in the Common Pleas: Further Studies", *Cambridge Law Journal*, i.

point."[1] Yet, as usual, the last thing that he wanted was to become involved in controversy. On the republication of his papers in book form, he was careful to stress in the preface, in a famous sentence, "it may be expedient for me to say that I am a dissenter from both, and from other Churches",[2] and the Lyndwood essay opened with disarming modesty—"It is likely that they are in the right and I am in the wrong. Nevertheless, the cause of truth may be served by the statement of an unfashionable opinion."[3] To Stubbs's feelings he was especially tender. Professor Cheney has accused him of being ungenerous in not quoting §389 of the *Constitutional History*, where Stubbs came to a more nearly correct account of the true position about the canon law in medieval England than he did in the *Report*.[4] This, however, is to disregard a footnote to the Lyndwood article as it originally appeared, in which Maitland said that, if there was a gradual change in view indicated by the *Constitutional History*, the two lectures on the medieval canon law, and the historical appendix, this seemed to him a change in the wrong direction.[5] This Maitland omitted from the reprint in *Roman Canon Law in the Church of England*, no doubt lest it should be hurtful to Stubbs— and so are men's efforts at kindliness represented as lack of generosity! Some little time after the book appeared Maitland wrote to Poole, "I hope and trust that you were not very serious when you said that the bishop was 'sore'."[6] He had far too high a regard for Stubbs's achievement willingly to offend him.[7]

[1] 23 Sept. 1895, *Letters*, p. 145.   [2] *R.C.L.*, p. vi.   [3] *ibid.*, p. 1.
[4] C. R. Cheney, *The English Church from Becket to Langton* (1956), p. 4.
[5] *E.H.R.*, xi, 447.   [6] 12 Sept. 1898, *Letters*, pp. 181–182.
[7] Stubbs was Maitland's senior by a quarter of a century; he was made Bishop of Chester in 1884 and translated to Oxford in 1889, so that the academic careers of the two men scarcely overlapped. They did not meet each other. "I never spoke to him," Maitland told Poole. "I never saw him but once, and that in church" (*Letters*, p. 225). All the same, in both his Rede Lecture and the obituary that Poole persuaded him to write for the *English Historical Review* in 1901, Maitland was not sparing in his praise of Stubbs. "In his power of marshalling legal details so as to bring to view some living principle or some phase of national development," Maitland told his Cambridge audience, "he has had no rival and no second among Englishmen" (*English Law and the Renaissance*, p. 19). Or again, in the obituary, "No other

Stubbs did not find it easy to change opinions once he had formed them—and perhaps it was especially hard for him to abandon a thesis in the making of which, he claimed in his lectures, he had "put together a mass of matter . . . both true history and the result of hard work".[1] Moreover, by 1898 he had "lost so much by translation",[2] and his Oxford diocesan commitments left him little time for an objective consideration of all that Maitland's work implied. His reference to the whole matter in a note in the 1900 edition of his *Seventeen Lectures* was not very satisfactory: it contained a formal acceptance of "any amount of adjustment of facts and authorities" that Maitland might prescribe, and a rather lame justification, if such it can be called, of his own position.[3]

Not all his supporters gave even as much ground as Stubbs was prepared to do.[4] Scholarly opinion, however, was, and is, on Maitland's side. H. J. Rashdall claimed for *Roman Canon Law in the Church of England* that the history of our medieval church would have to be rewritten in its light.[5] Maitland's own comment was utterly modest: writing to Fisher towards the end of his life, he said, "I got more fun out of that than out of any other job I ever did."[6]

Englishman has so completely displayed to the world the whole business of the historian from the winning of the new material to the narrating and generalising" (*C.P.*, iii, 498). More significant from the present point of view, in the obituary Maitland also said something of the personal influence that the *Constitutional History* had exercised over him—"I did not read it because I was set to read it, or because I was to be examined in it, or because I had to teach history or law. I found it in a London club, and read it because it was interesting" (*C.P.*, iii, 503). What has so much puzzled Mr Richardson and Professor Sayles—the long-continuing influence of the *Constitutional History* —is partly explicable in just those terms. It is an interesting book.

[1] W. Stubbs, *Seventeen Lectures on the Study of Medieval and Modern History*, 1886, p. 379.

[2] Hutton, *Letters of William Stubbs*, p. 300.

[3] Stubbs, *Seventeen Lectures*, 1900, p. 335.

[4] See A. Ogle, *The Canon Law in Medieval England*; Hutton, *Letters of William Stubbs*, p. 206; Malcolm MacColl, *The Reformation Settlement*, 8th edn., pp. 751–762.

[5] *E.H.R.*, xix (1904), 146.   [6] 6 Feb. 1905, *Letters*, p. 328.

IX

THE SIXTEENTH CENTURY

MAITLAND'S work on the sixteenth century is, of course, a great deal less in both bulk and significance than his medieval studies. Indeed, at first sight, there may seem to have been an element of the almost accidental about his penetration into the first of the "modern" centuries. It was his inquiries into the canon law, discussed in the last chapter, that turned his interests towards the English reformation, and it was the inspiration of Lord Acton that actualized those interests. Anxious to avoid the partisan writing of the acknowledged experts in reformation history, Acton issued the invitation which resulted in Maitland's chapter for the second volume of the *Cambridge Modern History*, "The Anglican Settlement and the Scottish Reformation". Judged superficially, this must have seemed a strange choice of contributor, and perhaps it appeared odder still that Maitland should have accepted the assignment. Certainly, with his habitual modesty, he was conscious that both invitation and acceptance would provoke comment, for when, in a letter unfortunately undated, he let Fisher into the secret, he urged discretion about it—"As for me I am going down for the Anglican System!—do not reveal this."[1]

Throughout 1898 he was involved in the heavy reading that his subject demanded, and references to it began to creep into his correspondence. By an interesting coincidence J. H. Round had also moved forward into the same period and subject, producing from 1897 onwards a series of characteristically controversial papers in the *Nineteenth Century Review* and the

---

[1] Maitland to Fisher, Bod., F.P., Box 27.

Contemporary Review.[1] With the conclusions of these Maitland was, broadly speaking, in sympathy, but, probably wisely, refused Round's invitation to contribute to a volume of essays that he was planning.[2] Round was, as Miss Cam has put it, "a Protestant of a very different kidney" from Maitland,[3] and his approach and method made him something of a lone wolf. "Are you well advised", Maitland asked him, "in seeking to form a team? Would not your own papers look better by themselves?"[4] Moreover—and in the present connection more significant—apart from the personal difficulties involved in an association with Round, Maitland showed no desire to become deeply committed to the sixteenth century. "I like most centuries better," he told Round.[5] That he found his chapter for the *Cambridge Modern History* an interesting assignment, and that he put a fantastic amount of work into it, is undeniable. But he was probably relieved when, by the summer of 1899, with the bulk of the work done and the chapter under revision, he was able to say, "just at present I keep Elizabeth for Sundays".[6] He had got the sixteenth century back into its place—not a very high one in his list of priorities.

Apart from its concern with a period with which he had not been associated, Maitland's chapter for the *Cambridge Modern History* was uncharacteristic of him in another way. It was the only excursion he ever made into straight narrative history, and there are not wanting references in his letters that make it clear that he was not overattracted to that sort of historical writing.[7] Indeed, there are sentences here and there in his correspondence that suggest that he was critical of the *Cambridge Modern History*,

[1] "The Elizabethan Religion", *Nineteenth Century Review*, 1897; "The Sacrifice of the Mass", *ibid.*; "Popular Church History", *Contemporary Review*, 1898; "As Established by Law", *ibid.*, 1899.

[2] 29 Dec. 1898, Maitland to Round, *Letters*, p. 186.

[3] *Essays*, p. xxi.

[4] 29 Dec. 1898, *Letters*, pp. 186–187.

[5] *ibid.*, p. 187.

[6] 7 July 1899, Maitland to Round, *ibid.*, p. 198.

[7] See above, pp. 10–11.

although Acton had consulted him at an early stage about its planning. "It will be a very strange book, that History of ours," he confessed to his friend, Henry Jackson.[1] Or, later on, writing regretfully about Fisher's failure to secure election to a professorship at Cambridge, "How you would have made that Camb.Mod.Hist. hum!" he said.[2] Perhaps most revealing of all, in another letter he wrote to Fisher, "Pray relieve the Cam.Mod. Hist. with an anecdote or two", he exhorted him.[3] Maitland's own techniques had been developed for the description and analysis of legal systems and institutions; he had no previous experience of detailed, chronologically unfolding, narrative history.

It is not surprising if some critics have felt that his chapter shows something of both his preference for the Middle Ages and his unfamiliarity with the writing of narrative history. As to the first, a number of passages can be cited where he seems to be looking nostalgically back to the earlier centuries. Sixteenth-century Scotland puts him in mind of the dark age, of Charles the Simple and Rolf the Pirate;[4] the nobles' doings in that age "send back our thoughts to far-off Carolingian days".[5] Or again, discussing the case that Henry II of France might make against Elizabeth's legitimacy, "That heretics are not to rule", he says, "was no new principle; the Counts of Toulouse had felt its edge in the old Albigensian days."[6] As to the second, some have held the view that Maitland's chapter is too tightly packed with fact and allusion, some of which—or at least its significance—tends to escape the reader. Partly this was due to the fact that the editors of the *Cambridge Modern History* had set their faces against footnotes, which prevented Maitland from showing his references. Partly, however, it resulted from his writing after a short, but very intensive, study of the sources, to which he was in a sense closer than most of his readers can ever hope to be.

[1] 18 Feb. 1900, *Letters*, p. 212.
[2] 16 Nov. 1903, Maitland to Fisher, *ibid.*, p. 286.
[3] 28 Sept. 1904, *ibid.*, p. 315.
[4] *C.M.H.*, ii, 553.   [5] *ibid.*, p. 554.
[6] *ibid.*, p. 560.

Whatever the reason, there is substance in Sir Maurice Powicke's criticism that "this fine *tour de force* needs a commentary".[1]

Yet, when these things have been said, it must be added that Maitland's chapter is a notably distinguished piece of historical writing. Certainly of all the chapters in the old Cambridge Modern History it is the most readable and memorable. Once they have caught the eye, Maitland's effective and epigrammatic summaries of a situation can scarcely be forgotten: without conscious effort by the reader they pass into his mind and become, in a very special way, part of his own intellectual property.[2] An interesting example of this is Mr Conyers Read's study of Anglo-Scottish relations in *Mr. Secretary Cecil and Queen Elizabeth*, where on at least two occasions he uses Maitland's actual phrases. This is not intentional plagiarism: it is simply that there is a quality of inescapability about Maitland's way of putting things.[3]

Nor is the virtue of the chapter only in its detail. Even more remarkable is the confident control of his material that enabled Maitland to fuse the two topics that he treated, the Scottish reformation and the Elizabethan church settlement, and to bring out the long-term significance of both. So it is that of the relationship of Knox and Elizabeth he says, "They did not love each other; but she had saved his Scottish Reformation, and he had

[1] *Journal of Ecclesiastical History*, ix (1958), 248.

[2] Some examples, taken at random, may be given—

After the capitulation of 1547, "John Knox was shipped off with the rest, and was kept in the galleys for nineteen months, to meditate on faith that justifies" (*C.M.H.*, ii, 556).

The battle of Pinkie, "No more decisive defeat could have been inflicted on the Scottish host and the Brittanic idea" (*ibid*, p. 557).

The peace of Edinburgh, "Perhaps the truest victory that England had won was over herself. Not a word had been publicly said of that old suzerainty; no spoil had been taken, not a town detained" (*ibid.*, p. 577).

[3] Conyers Read, p. 136, "Indeed Knox had narrowly escaped the bishopric of Rochester"; Maitland, *C.M.H.*, ii, 557, "John Knox . . . had narrowly escaped the bishopric of Rochester." Conyers Read, p. 127, "Elizabeth herself probably perceived that there was nothing to be gained by mere schism"; Maitland, *C.M.H.*, ii, 563, "But in 1558 nothing was to be gained by mere schism."

saved her Anglican Settlement";[1] and so he summarizes the
trend of the period he has described, "Two kingdoms are drifting
together, first towards a 'personal' and then towards a 'real'
Union; but two churches are drifting apart into dissension and
antagonism."[2]

As to the content of the chapter, what Maitland wrote about
the Scottish reformation and about Anglo-Scottish relations is
best read alongside the relevant parts of Mr Conyers Read's
volume;[3] this, however, glosses and expands, rather than super-
sedes, Maitland. Indeed, apart from some doubt amongst Scottish
historians as to whether he did not exaggerate the backwardness
of the country,[4] this part of Maitland's work has stood firm. The
same is not true of his description of the Elizabethan church
settlement and of the circumstances in which its foundations, the
Acts of Supremacy and Uniformity, were laid. In that connection
the more recent, and quite contrary, thesis of Sir John Neale has
commanded acceptance.[5]

Maitland's interpretation of the parliamentary history of
9 February to 29 April 1559 was that Elizabeth was farther to the
left in religion than many of her subjects, that her attempt to
change church services was resisted and abandoned, and that the
Prayer Book of 1552 with very few changes was introduced as a
short way of settling the matter, and one that could be claimed as
an act of restoration. Professor Neale, on the other hand, argues
that the queen's real desire was to take the line of little by little
that had been recommended by Armagil Waad at the very outset
of her reign—that is, to obtain initially simply an Act of
Supremacy, to use that to get rid of recalcitrant bishops, and then
to pass a prayer book through convocation before bringing it to
a second parliament. The indication that this was Elizabeth's
intention he finds in the clause, at first sight oddly embedded in

---

[1] *C.M.H.*, ii, 580.   [2] *ibid.*, p. 590.

[3] *Mr. Secretary Cecil and Queen Elizabeth* (1955), chs. VII, VIII, XI.

[4] G. Donaldson, *The Scottish Reformation* (1960), p. 75.

[5] J. E. Neale, "The Elizabethan Acts of Supremacy and Uniformity",
E.H.R., lxv (1950); *Elizabeth and her Parliaments*, 1559–81, part I, chs. II
and III.

the Act of Supremacy, that there should be communion in both kinds: certainly this does seem to imply that she did not originally intend any Act of Uniformity. According to the Neale thesis, the demand for that came from the commons, and the radical features of the settlement derived not, as Maitland thought, from the queen, but from a pressure group of some hundred or more M.P.s, with a core of twelve to sixteen returned exiles,[1] led by Cecil's father-in-law, Sir Anthony Cooke, Sir Nicholas Bacon and Sir Francis Knollys, and backed by Cox, Sandys, Grindal, Horne, Jewel and Scory as their spiritual advisers. Despite the heavy amendments the commons made in the government's Supremacy Bill, Elizabeth meant to push it through; the lords deleted the amendments and returned it to the commons more or less in its original form; by them it was agreed and was ready for the royal assent on 22 March. At that point, however, the queen had second thoughts. The conclusion of the peace of Cateau Cambrésis freed her hands, the tough tactics of the commons prevailed: on 24 March she changed her mind, adjourned instead of proroguing parliament, "and, in so doing, altered the pattern of the Elizabethan religious settlement".[2]

There were some interesting by-products of Maitland's chapter. In December 1899 his *Fortnightly Review* article demolished wittily and conclusively the existence of a convocation of the clergy by which, according to Canon MacColl, the Act of Uniformity was passed. Then again, between 1900 and 1903 there appeared in the *English Historical Review* his "Elizabethan Gleanings". The first of them was the famous note on the " &c." which, in the early months of her reign, Elizabeth used in her title instead of "Supreme Head of the Church of England", to which she lacked statutory claim—"Then a happy thought occurs. Let her highness etceterate herself."[3] Alas, as Maitland's

---

[1] Conyers Read points out that a comparison of Garrett's list of the exiles with the official returns to the commons of 1559 makes it appear that only nine were elected (*Mr. Secretary Cecil and Queen Elizabeth*, p. 480 note 29.)

[2] *Elizabeth and her Parliaments, 1559–81*, p. 69.

[3] *C.P.*, iii, 159.

friend Hubert Hall was later to show, this was merely to revive
a precedent of Mary Tudor.[1] Three of the other papers were
based either on Froude's Spanish transcripts or on the Roman
transcripts that had recently been undertaken for the Master of
the Rolls and were available in the Public Record Office. Finally,
and most important, there was an article, characteristic of Maitland in its shrewd observation of detail, on the diplomatic of the
Acts of Settlement and Uniformity: as early as October 1899 he
had written to Poole, "If I have to sing a Nunc dimittis it will run
'quid oculi mei viderunt originalem Actum de Uniformitate
primi anni Reg.Eliz.' ",[2] and as late as four years after there is
surviving correspondence about his visiting the Victoria Tower
to see the originals of the acts.[3]

While his work on the Elizabethan religious settlement was in
progress, Maitland was invited to give the Rede Lecture at
Cambridge in 1901. Sir Robert Rede was a Tudor judge, and it
was appropriate that Maitland should take the law of sixteenth-
century England as his subject. The lines he was to follow in this
lecture he had already sketched out three years before in his
English Historical Review notice of *The Records of the Honourable
Society of Lincoln's Inn*:

> What was it [he asked in that review] that saved English law when
> the day of strain and trial came in the sixteenth century? Why was
> there in England no "reception" of Roman Law? We ought to
> pause before we answer these questions. We ought to look not
> only at Germany, but also at France and Scotland. The danger was
> very great. In "the new monarchy", as Mr Green called it, the
> monarch must often have felt that his legal tools were clumsy, and
> there were plenty of people to tell him where to look for apter
> instruments. As it was, our common law had a bad time under
> Henry VIII. In all directions its provenance was being narrowed
> by the new courts, the Star Chamber, the Court of Requests, the
> Council of the North, and so forth. There comes a moment when
> the stream of law reports, which has been flowing ever since the
> time of Edward I, seems to be on the very point of running dry.
> Reginald Pole, the highly educated young man who is not far

[1] *Fortnightly Review*, 2 May 1908.
[2] 8 Oct. 1899, *Letters*, p. 201.
[3] C.U. MS. 7007, nos. 223 and 227.

from the throne, is saying that the time has come for Roman law: every well-ruled nation is adopting it. The Protector Somerset is keenly interested in getting a great "civil law college" founded at Cambridge. To praise "the civil law" is a mark of enlightenment, and sometimes of advanced protestantism, for your common lawyer is apt to be medievally and even popishly inclined.[1]

For Maitland there was one fact that accounted for the survival of the common law, and it was that fact which had led him to introduce these ideas into a review of a book about Lincoln's Inn. What gave the common law its toughness was that, for generations, it had been formally taught in the Inns of Court. It was a tough, taught law that was able, if only just able, to ward off the threat of a Reception.

Published under the title *English Law and the Renaissance*, and dedicated to James Bradley Thayer, a professor in the Harvard Law School and honorary secretary for America of the Selden Society, Maitland's Rede Lecture developed the points made in his review. Charmingly presented and infinitely persuasive though the lecture is, it is doubtful whether any legal historian familiar with the period would today accept its thesis that in Henry VIII's reign the common law was seriously endangered and a Reception of Roman law at that time well within the bounds of possibility. The reasons for this rejection are most apparent if we look at the four main bases of Maitland's argument —(i) that this period saw a decline in the business of the common-law courts and, contemporary with that decline, a European-wide revival of the civil law; (ii) that the long series of Year Books, a tradition more than two centuries old of law reporting, came to an end in 1535; (iii) that the new, so-called prerogative courts of Tudor England threatened the common law; (iv) that Henry VIII had despotic inclinations.

(i) It seems likely that Maitland exaggerated the extent to which a decline of the common-law courts took place. Holdsworth's statistical tables of the number of rolls of these courts, and of the numbers of cases on them,[2] indicate that business

---

[1] *E.H.R.*, xiii (1898), 576.
[2] *History of English Law*, iv, 255–256.

continued regularly and, in Elizabeth's reign, was even subject to a large increase; this suggests that any falling-off there may have been was not sufficient to be regarded as constituting a serious and permanent threat. It is true that, specifically for King's Bench, Miss Blatcher has shown a shrinkage of the Rex roll, which recorded criminal business; that decline, she reckons, amounted to something like half to two-thirds between the last terms of Henry VII's reign and the 1530s and early '40s, and she may be right in associating it with the competition of the conciliar courts and, so far as treason is concerned, of special commissions.[1] Also, on the plea side, she prints figures that leave the impression of decline and claims that most of its small amount of business was the product of its ingenuity in connection with Bills of Middlesex and *Latitats*.[2] Yet is not the creation of a fiction of the sort involved in these itself indicative of a lively and resilient court?

Nor should the practical effects of the civil-law revival be antedated. Alciati, Zäsi, Budé, Hotman, Cujas and others made the sixteenth century a period of notable renovation of the Roman law; but the careers of only the first three belong to the first half of the century, and Maitland admitted that the great Frenchmen who did so much for the revival were, in the 1530s, still youthful or unborn.[3] In any event the leaning of the first humanist lawyers was naturally academic, and in the meantime the law practised in the courts of Germany and France, still in the Bartolist tradition, was every bit as much riddled with technicality as the English common law.[4] If that was the Euro-

---

[1] Dr Hunnisett, however, has pointed out to me that, by the Tudor period, the Rex section of the *coram rege* roll is much less representative of the work of the court than it had been in the Middle Ages. The real test of the amount of the court's work on that side is in ancient indictments and the controlment rolls, which show that only a small proportion of cases is enrolled on the Rex roll.

[2] Marjorie Blatcher, "Touching the Writ of Latitat: an Act 'Of No Great Moment' " in *Elizabethan Government and Society*, ed. S. T. Bindoff, J. Hurstfield, C. H. Williams (1961), pp. 199–201.

[3] *E.L.Ren.*, p. 6.

[4] Holdsworth, *H.E.L.*, iv, 260.

pean background, in England itself the civil lawyers do not seem
to have been very influential. As early as 1896 Maitland claimed
that too little had been written of the English civilians of the
sixteenth century;[1] but though individual civil lawyers like
Layton and Legh occupied political positions of importance
under Henry VIII, in the properly legal sphere the civil law
operated in only two areas—after 1538 it was practised in the
ecclesiastical courts and, because the court of admiralty was
concerned with foreigners, it was the law of that court, too.[2]

(ii) Maitland thought it peculiarly sinister that, in 1535, the
last of the Year Books appeared—"The exact significance of this
ominous event", he said, "has never yet been duly explored;
but ominous it surely is."[3] Yet how seriously the end of the Year
Books should be taken is open to question. Their last period
showed no decline in significance—Lord Keeper Guilford, indeed, at the end of the seventeenth century, chose to begin his
study of them with the Year Books of Henry VII, because it was
then that the common law, after previous fluctuations, became
really settled.[4] As for their actual termination, that mattered less
because the private reports immediately succeeded, and indeed
overlapped, them. Mr Brian Simpson has pointed out that the
so-called *Keilwey's Reports* bear such a close resemblance to the
Year Books that some of the Year Books themselves may have
originated as private productions, not different in kind from the
later works of Dyer and Plowden.[5] The Year Books, after all,
had never been an official publication, and it is not convincing
to represent their end as being due to Machiavellian government
action.

(iii) At a time when the Whig interpretation of history still
held the field, it was no doubt the most telling of Maitland's
arguments that prerogative courts threatened the common law.
"Might not the Council and the Star Chamber and the Court

---

[1] *R.C.L.*, p. 94.
[2] G. R. Elton, *The Tudor Constitution* (1960), p. 152.
[3] *E.L.Ren.*, p. 22.
[4] Roger North, *Lives of the Norths* (ed. Jessop, 1890), i, 26.
[5] *L.Q.R.*, lxxiii (1957), 105.

of Requests", he said, "—courts not tied and bound by ancient formalism—do the romanizing work that was done in Germany by the Imperial Chamber Court, the *Reichskammergericht*?"[1] The answer, I suppose, is that they might have done, but that in practice they did not.

For one thing, their popularity was fluctuating. Initially their procedures were summary, simple and—so far as the court of requests was concerned—cheap. But quite rapidly complications and dilatoriness developed, and so, if we are to believe the chronicler, Hall, after Wolsey's fall from power they went into at least a temporary decline. "These courtes", he says, "were greatly haunted for a tyme, but at the last the people perceaued that much delay was used in these courtes & few matters ended, & when they were ended, they bound no man by the law; then euery man was wery of them & resorted to the common law."[2]

Again, while Maitland seized on any Roman law elements in the prerogative courts (for instance, Sir Julius Caesar's statement that the procedure of the court of requests "was altogether according to the process of summary causes in the Ciuill Law"), he markedly neglected the strong common-law influences to which all the prerogative courts were subject. The most notable of these was perhaps the matter of personnel. A nominal roll of eleven members of Henry VII's council learned in the law lists eight common lawyers;[3] amongst those reckoned judges in star chamber were the two chief justices and the chief baron of the three common-law courts;[4] despite the predominance of civilians among the masters of requests, the court of requests had always, from Cromwell's time, one common lawyer on its staff,[5] and, considerably earlier, the Sir Robert Rede, whose lecture Maitland gave, himself sat on occasion as a judge of the court. It is worth nothing that the Tudor chancery had a similar

[1] *E.L.Ren.*, pp. 19–20.

[2] Cited in *Select Cases in the Court of Requests*, Selden Soc., vol. 12, p. xiv.

[3] *Select Cases in the Council of Henry VII*, Selden Soc., vol. 75, p. xxv.

[4] *Select Cases before the King's Council in the Star Chamber*, Selden Soc., vol. 16, pp. xxv, seq.

[5] Elton, *T.R.H.S.*, 5th series, vi (1956), p. 79.

common-law element in its personnel—except during Mary's reign, Tudor chancellors were normally common lawyers. Nor did the financial courts differ from this pattern—the lord chief justice and the attorney-general were put on a fixed salary in the court of surveyors in 1544, and their services had, in fact, been used before that;[1] in the augmentations the postion was similar;[2] and in the court of wards the three senior common-law judges were regularly paid fees as judge's assistant.[3] A proclamation of 1546 provided that no one might plead in these courts without previously reading in one of the Inns, unless he had been specially appointed by the chancellor and the two chief justices with the advice of the benchers of the Inns.[4]

Even regarding procedure, it is possible to exaggerate the contrast between the prerogative and the common-law courts. On the one hand, procedure by examination, so characteristic of the former, had, in fact, been making its way into the common-law courts during the fifteenth century;[5] on the other, examples are not wanting where star-chamber procedure followed that of the common law.[6] It is true that the common lawyers were jealous of the new ideas and new developments, and reacted sharply against them.[7] The conflict of jurisdictions, however, needs to be properly understood. It belonged rather to the last decades of the sixteenth century than to the 'thirties and 'forties, and, when it did come, was less a matter of principle than cut-throat competition for business.

[1] W. C. Richardson, *History of the Court of Augmentations 1536–1554* (1961), p. 388.

[2] *ibid.*, pp. 389–390.

[3] Bell, *Introduction to the History and Records of the Court of Wards and Liveries*, p. 98.

[4] Holdsworth, *H.E.L.*, iv, 271.

[5] *Select Cases in the Council of Henry VII*, Selden Soc., vol. 75, p. liii.

[6] *Select Cases before the King's Council in the Star Chamber*, Selden Soc., vol. 16.

[7] See, for example, "*A Replication of a Serjaunte at the Lawe of England*" in Francis Hargrave, *A Collection of Tracts relative to the Law of England* (1787), i, 321–331; Appeal of the common lawyers, *Acts of the Privy Council*, 1547–1550, pp. 48–50.

(iv) The Victorian view that Thomas Cromwell was consciously seeking to establish a tyranny for Henry VIII was one
into which Maitland could fit his thesis of a threatened reception
of Roman law. "There was pleasant reading in the Byzantine
Code," he put it, "for a king who wished to be monarch in
church as well as state, pleasanter reading than could be found
in our ancient English law-books."[1] On the whole, however, it
is true to say that the interpretation of Cromwell's rule, accepted
by many of Maitland's contemporaries, has today been abandoned by most historians of the period. It has, it is true, found
one supporter in Mr Laurence Stone, who sees both parliament
and common law in danger of extinction in the period.[2] His
case, however, is less convincing than that of Dr G. R. Elton,
who claims that Cromwell deserves the title of England's first
parliamentary statesman and that, so far as the prerogative
courts threatened the old common-law courts, they did so as
bodies that were able to enforce the common law more effectively.[3] However it may be as to the issue between these two,
on one specific point Maitland was clearly wrong: his conjecture
that the proposed erection of a court of "Justices or Conservators
of the Common Weal" constituted a threat to the common
law must have been made because he used the calendar only and
not the text of the original document, since the text makes it
clear that that court was to proceed by due course of common
law.[4]

An examination of Maitland's principal arguments in *English
Law and the Renaissance* in the light of work done on Tudor
legal history since his death makes it impossible to uphold the
lecture's central thesis. To say that, however, is not to deny the
stimulating quality of this piece of his work, nor to deny that its
inspirational value proved very great. Especially in the extended
notes that, on publication, he added to the lecture, he provided

---

[1] *E.L.Ren.*, p. 14.

[2] "The Political Programme of Thomas Cromwell", *B.I.H.R.*, (1951), xxiv.

[3] "The Political Creed of Thomas Cromwell", *T.R.H.S.*, 5th series, vi (1956).

[4] Plucknett, "Some Proposed Legislation of Henry VIII", *T.R.H.S.*, 4th
series, xix (1936).

for his successors a mass of hints that they have not been slow to use for the better understanding of sixteenth-century legal development.

On a number of occasions in this book, indications have been given of the way in which Maitland came to the subjects that he studied and of how he effected the transition from one to another. One final sixteenth-century topic on which he worked remains to be mentioned and set in context in that sort of way. In his Rede lecture he had occasion to speak of Sir Thomas Smith, the first holder of Henry VIII's professorship of civil law at Cambridge. For a moment he turned aside to glance at Smith's important tract, the *De Republica Anglorum*—

> The little treatise on the Commonwealth of England which he wrote at Toulouse in 1565—a remarkable feat for he had no English books at hand—became a classic in the next century, and certainly did not underrate those traditional, medieval, Germanic and parliamentary elements which were still to be found in English life and law under the fifth and last of the Tudors.[1]

Maitland's interest aroused, entirely typically he began to think in terms of the Selden Society doing an edition of Smith; equally typically, in the course of the resultant discussions, Pollock poured cold water on the plan—surely, he thought, the *De Republica Anglorum* was too modern for the Selden Society.[2] In the upshot the edition was prepared by Maitland's pupil, L. Alston, and published by the Cambridge University Press: Maitland contributed a preface to the volume, and, apart from that, its editor later made a handsome acknowledgment to Fisher as to the large share his professor had had in the work.[3]

It cannot be claimed that Maitland, either by inclination or achievement, was a Tudor historian. Nevertheless, his two principal sixteenth-century studies were more than mere postscripts to the medieval scholarship on which his reputation rests, for both stood in a recognizable, structural relationship to that work.

[1] *E.L.Ren.*, p. 16.
[2] 22 June, 1904, Pollock to Maitland, C.U. MS. 7007.
[3] 4 June 1909, Alston to Fisher, Bod., F.P., Box 27.

The Church of England, after all, entered into an inheritance that was, in some important ways, both medieval and catholic—even if the nature of that inheritance was misunderstood by the Anglicans of the Oxford Movement. As for the common law, the early development of which Maitland had described with such artistry and skill, much of its medieval forms and practice was still vigorously alive in 1600. "Coke's books", as he said, "are the great dividing line, and we are hardly out of the Middle Ages till he has dogmatized its results."[1] Tudor England was the frontier territory of a land that, perhaps more than any other man, Maitland had made his own.

[1] S. E. Thorne, *Sir Edward Coke* (Selden Society Lecture, 1952), p. 5.

MAITLAND AS TEACHER

In 1901 W. A. J. Archbold edited a volume entitled *Essays on the Teaching of History*, for which Acton had agreed to write an introduction. On his death Maitland took over the task, and his introductory essay, though not in itself especially distinguished, does contain an interesting, and characteristically generous, appreciation of the teacher's work. "When all men get their due", he wrote, "a large share of credit will be given to those whose patient and self-denying labours as tutors and lecturers have left them little time for the acquisition of such fame as may be won by great books."[1] The tone of this is that of a commentator from outside, and it is clear that Maitland did not regard himself as an influential, dedicated teacher. That assessment is only partly just. It is true that he lacked experience of that tutorial work which, at Oxford and Cambridge, most of all makes teaching reputations: at the time of life when many are at their most effective as tutors[2] he was away from Cambridge, practising at the Bar, and he never, indeed, occupied the position of a college supervisor. On the other hand, as reader, and later as Downing Professor, he lectured with distinction over a wide range of legal and historical topics for a period of twenty years. Even during the latter part of his life, when his health forced him to spend each Lent term in the Canaries, he scrupulously completed the balance of his lecturing commitment by offering courses during the Long Vacation term.

The lecture courses that Maitland gave fall into two separate

---

[1] *Essays on the Teaching of History* (1901), p. xvii; reprinted in *C.P.*, iii.
[2] A. H. Smith, *Selected Essays and Addresses* (1963), p. 31.

categories—on the one hand, those designed as straight teaching for the law tripos, pointed to the needs of the ordinary under-graduate candidate for the tripos; on the other, those that were of more specialist character, often the forerunner, and sometimes the by-product, of his books. It is well to say something of each group.

The first kind of lectures was especially his preoccupation during the years 1885–1888, when he held the readership—a period in which he advertised courses on tort,[1] on real property,[2] on the rise and progress of the laws of England,[3] on Stephen's *Commentaries*,[4] and, above all, the lectures on constitutional history.[5] But even after his election to the professorship he never neglected this run-of-the-mill teaching work. During his tenure of the chair his courses included personal property,[6] constitutional law and history,[7] contract,[8] advanced real property,[9] a general sketch of English legal history,[10] some points in the law of real property,[11] an introduction to the study of English law,[12] and the lectures on equity. The last-mentioned, constantly revised and expanded from a one-term into a two-term course, he delivered every year from 1892 to 1906. Much of this lecturing involved Maitland in routine work of preparation that some—A. F. Pollard among them[13]—have regarded as a waste of talents that they feel should have been wholly devoted to original scholarship and research, and even Maitland himself occasionally expressed regret at the time that they consumed. "For weeks", he told

---

[1] Mich. 1885.
[2] Lent and Easter 1886, Easter 1887, Easter 1888.
[3] Mich. 1886.
[4] Lent 1887, Mich. 1887.
[5] Lent and Easter, 1888.
[6] Easter 1889.
[7] Mich. 1889 and Lent 1890.
[8] Mich. 1889, Long Vac. and Mich. 1901.
[9] Lent 1890, Lent 1892.
[10] Mich. 1893, Mich. 1894.
[11] Easter 1895, Long Vac. 1903, *do.* 1904, *do.* 1905, *do.* 1906.
[12] Mich. 1900, Mich. 1901, Long Vac. 1902.
[13] *Morning Post*, 20 July 1911, reviewing *C.P.*

Pollock in 1887, "I have been in horrible bondage to my lectures. Stephen's chapters about the Royal Prerogatives and so forth . . . are a terrible struggle."[1] But their significance was that a long generation of Cambridge law students came under Maitland's spell and learnt that the law is not just a livelihood but, in some ways, a calling, too. Of course, amongst those who attended there were men who were later to become distinguished academic lawyers—from the early days Edward Jenks, and later on W. J. Whittaker, professor at University College, London, and Professor H. A. Hollond, whose long career was to be in Cambridge. There was, too, one man destined to become an outstandingly great statesman: in supplying Smuts with a testimonial, Maitland, with an enthusiastic assessment of the young South African's abilities, told him that he might become "the great Romanist, the Ihering of English Law".[2] Nevertheless, the most important influence of these lectures was perhaps on those who were, as barristers or solicitors, to be the ordinary practitioners of the law: it was on behalf of these men that Whittaker spoke so movingly at the memorial meeting on 1 June 1907.[3]

That we possess direct evidence about these lectures, and do not depend solely on the impressions of those who attended them, is due to Maitland's brother-in-law, H. A. L. Fisher, who, after Maitland's death, decided to arrange the publication of the courses on constitutional history, on equity, and (perhaps best of all) on the forms of action. This was not a decision easily reached, for Maitland himself, though on occasion admitting that some of his lectures could be prepared for the press with relative ease, had more often expressed an unwillingness to publish them. "Fred had a great dislike to publishing lectures—or rather a great reticence or unwillingness to do so", Mrs Maitland informed her brother. "Often I used to tell him that his best sets ought to be published and he always replied that they were not in a fit state for publication and would need months and months of work as a

[1] 12 Nov. 1887, *Letters*, p. 35.
[2] W. K. Hancock, *Smuts* (1962), i, 46.
[3] *Cambridge University Reporter*, 22 July 1907.

great deal of them was merely notes to lecture from."[1] Such editing as the constitutional history lectures required, which was in any event not much, Fisher himself provided, while those on equity and the forms of action, which did present more problems, were handled by A. H. Chaytor and W. J. Whittaker. Some of Maitland's most ardent admirers have felt it a pity that these posthumously published books should have been more read than his works of original scholarship. Certainly they lack the profound learning of those and, more curiously, their lightness of touch—what his friend Buckland called "the play of fancy and the humour which ornament his other work".[2] Flashes of both are there;[3] but, comparatively speaking, they are few and far between. Nevertheless, the number of reprints into which these posthumous volumes have run[4] provides the justification for Fisher's decision: Maitland's capacity for the organization of historical and legal facts makes his printed lectures *par excellence* students' books.

The second category of his lectures—those of more specialized subject-matter—is closely linked to the progress of his own scholarly interests: there is, indeed, a notable correlation between the dating of lecture courses of this sort and that of the publication of his books. Thus it can hardly be a coincidence that for Michaelmas term 1888 he announced a course on parliament and in January of the year following undertook the editing of a volume of parliamentary petitions for the Rolls Series. An even clearer connection, his lectures on the history of the English manor, were delivered for the first time in the Lent term of

[1] Undated, Mrs Maitland to Fisher, Bod., F.P., Box 27.

[2] *C.L.J.*, i, 287.

[3] e.g. *Equity*, p. 44—"Where judges and text-writers fear to tread professors of law have to rush in"; *ibid.*, p. 271—"It is only in novels, and in novels written by ladies, that the mortgagee's hand is stayed at the last moment by some god out of the machine."

[4] For *The Constitutional History of England* see p. 56 above; *Equity also The Forms of Action at Common Law* was published in 1909, and there were reprints in 1910, 1913, 1916, 1920, 1926, 1929, 1932, with a second edition edited by John Brunyate, 1936; *The Forms of Action at Common Law* was separately issued in 1936, and a paper-back edition appeared in 1962.

1889,[1] the year in which he was engaged in producing his Selden Society volume, *Select Pleas in Manorial Courts*. From 1891 to 1894 there followed a series of courses that were obviously a preparatory sortation of material for the *History of English Law*,[2] while the next year he announced lectures on the elementary history of the canon law, the preparation of which he confessed to having neglected for the studies that led to his *Roman Canon Law in the Church of England*.[3] In much the same way, his courses on the English village community[4] and agrarian Cambridge[5] are connected with his borough studies, just as the lectures he advertised for Michaelmas 1899, but through ill health had to cancel, reflect his mounting interest in the corporate personality. One specialist class he conducted repeatedly: that was the seminar in medieval handwriting.[6]

Classes and lectures of this kind, unlike lectures more directly relevant to the tripos, did not, of course, have a wide appeal: they were inevitably for the few, and it was no doubt of this side of Maitland's work that Oscar Browning was thinking when he commented—"His lectures were never numerously attended, at least not in my experience. More than half of the scanty audience were women; there was perhaps one undergraduate law student, then a few B.A.s and four or five historians from King's."[7] The small numbers did not matter, but what is odd and disappointing is Maitland's failure to find among them even a few disciples to prosecute the studies that were so near his heart. That he founded no school and had no following of research pupils—for Mary Bateson was lonely not merely in her eminence—has surprised and puzzled his admirers. Some have put it down, angrily, to the

---

[1] Given again in Mich. 1890.

[2] England law in the 13th century, Lent 1891; England land law in and before 1086, Mich. 1891; history of English law, cents. XII and XIII, introduction and tenure, Mich. 1892; *do.*, status and jurisdiction, Lent 1893; history of English land law, Mich. 1893; history of English law, cents. XII and XIII, Lent 1894.

[3] See above, p. 112.   [4] Mich. 1896.

[5] Lent, 1898.

[6] Mich. 1893, Mich. 1894, Mich. 1903, Mich. 1904, Mich. 1905.

[7] *Saturday Review*, 10 Sept. 1910.

heavy burden of undergraduate teaching borne by the professor
at an English university, leaving him too little time for the
organization of research; others, regretfully, to the bad health
that so hampered him throughout his career. In all probability
neither explanation is valid. Perhaps the key to the problem lies
in some remarks that Maitland made at a meeting held in 1900 to
promote a memorial to Henry Sidgwick. He spoke of Sidgwick's
marked dislike for any mere reproduction of his own opinions.
"I sometimes think," he said, "that the one and only prejudice
Sidgwick had was a prejudice against his own results."[1] Would
this not be true of Maitland himself? It may be that he lacked the
element of patronage, benign but basically authoritarian, that is
characteristic of the relationship between the professor and his
research pupil, and that he found co-operation in scholarship
easier with colleagues and co-evals than with juniors. It was
typical that in the last months of his life he offered to read the
proofs of Fisher's volume in the Longman *History of England*,[2]
and from that time, too, dates the hard work that he put into
J. W. Clark's edition of the *Liber Memorandum Ecclesie de Bernewelle*: indeed, he returned the final proof the day before he set out
on his final visit to the Canaries.[3]

For the rest, Maitland did not shirk any of the peripheral duties
of the university teacher. Although he did not, like Holdsworth,
positively enjoy examining, he took a full share of that work,
acting five times as examiner in the law tripos, three times in the
moral sciences tripos, and twice in the historical tripos.[4] From
November 1886 to January 1895 he was secretary of the University Law Board,[5] and from 1889 until 1901 of the Cambridge
Law Club:[6] to that club he read a final paper on the year books
and plea rolls just before leaving England for the last time.[7]

[1] A.S. and E.M.S., *Henry Sidgwick, a Memoir* (1906), pp. 305–306.
[2] 21 Sept. 1906, Maitland to Fisher, Bod., F.P., Box 27.
[3] J. W. Clark, *Liber Memorandum Ecclesie de Bernewelle* (1907), p. v.
[4] *Sketch*, p. 66.
[5] *ibid.*
[6] *C.P.*, iii, 419.
[7] 11 July 1910, A. P. Higgins to Fisher, Bod., F.P., Box 27.

INDEX

INDEX